WHEN THE
New Deal
CAME TO TOWN

A SNAPSHOT OF A PLACE AND TIME
WITH LESSONS FOR TODAY

GEORGE MELLOAN
ILLUSTRATIONS BY MOLLY MELLOAN

THRESHOLD EDITIONS

NEW YORK   LONDON   TORONTO   SYDNEY   NEW DELHI

Threshold Editions
An Imprint of Simon & Schuster, Inc.
1230 Avenue of the Americas
New York, NY 10020

First Threshold Editions hardcover edition November 2016

THRESHOLD EDITIONS and colophon are trademarks of Simon & Schuster,
Inc.

For information about special discounts for bulk purchases, please
contact Simon & Schuster Special Sales at 1-866-506-1949 or business@
simonandschuster.com.

The Simon & Schuster Speakers Bureau can bring authors to your live event.
For more information, or to book an event, contact the Simon & Schuster
Speakers Bureau at 1-866-248-3049 or visit our website at www.simonspeakers.com.

Manufactured in the United States of America

10   9   8   7   6   5   4   3   2   1

Library of Congress Cataloging-in-Publication Data is available.

ISBN 978-1-5011-3608-5
ISBN 978-1-5011-3610-8 (ebook)

In memory of my wife, Joan

CONTENTS

FOREWORD

Iт's not necessary to doubt the clear superiority of a truly republican form of government to acknowledge a self-evident truth: Even democratically elected leaders and representatives sometimes err. It is equally evident that when Washington makes mistakes, they often are big ones, affecting the lives of millions of citizens.

A recent example was the 2010 Affordable Care Act, unpopular because it did not live up to its promise of lower health care costs, raising them instead for much of the middle class. Then there was the Federal Reserve's zero-bound interest rate policy, which starved savers and pension funds of a decent return and facilitated a governmental spending spree that doubled the national debt in seven years.

This book examines a whole string of what we now know were political errors made in the early 1930s by first a Republican president and Congress and then by their Democratic successors, with an unhelpful central bank in a supporting role. Those mistakes veered the nation perilously close to the fascism that was then the politics du jour in much of Europe, to the world's eventual and extreme sorrow.

The 2008 and 1929 market crashes were both preceded by credit booms. The debt bubble that preceded the 2008 debacle began forming in 2002. From that year until the autumn of 2007, the amount of money raised in the U.S. credit markets nearly doubled, rising to an annual rate of $2,742 trillion from $1,398 trillion. It was fostered mainly by government efforts to promote home ownership by promoting mortgage loans to buyers with limited means.

The heavy borrowing of the 1920s was different. It was generated in large part by a remarkable era of innovation and the advent of "installment plan" buying that put new products within easier reach. Americans snapped up cars, cabinet radios, and such new labor-savers as electric vacuum cleaners and washing machines.

Home sales also surged, hitting a peak in 1925. Household indebtedness went from 15 percent of GDP in 1920 to 32 percent in 1929. As Irving Fisher, a leading economist of the time, observed, debt is deflationary. At some point, people have to stop buying and start paying off their debts. Consumption slows down, and instead of too much money chasing too few goods (inflation), not enough money is chasing too many goods (deflation). That, more than any other cause, accounted for the 1930s slump and its counterpart in 2008. The resulting economic slowdowns brought in radical governments that interfered with the market economy with damaging results.

Tons of words have been written about the Great Depression and its causes and effects by scores of economists and political scientists. But I thought it would be interesting to tell the story from the point of view not of policy makers or policy revisionists but of the rural people whose lives were subject to the policies. Interestingly enough, they often supported laws that would cost them dearly. There may be a lesson in that for our modern times, which are generating many of the anxieties that plagued the country back then.

The locale for this examination is a small farm town in Indiana called Whiteland, which I happen to know well because it's where I grew up. This is not a "victims" book. We all know that there were many victims, but their stories have been widely recorded—and sometimes exaggerated for political purposes. Rather it's the story of how life went on, people coped with economic adversity, and the system of checks and balances that America's forefathers designed passed a rigorous test. Special praise goes to the judicial branch, particularly the Supreme Court, which helped us through that trying period.

The people of Whiteland of that era didn't know that they were living through what would someday be described as a national disaster. They mainly knew it only as daily life. I suspect that was pretty much true of most Americans, other than those substantial numbers who found themselves in truly desperate straits. For the majority, life changed, but in subtle, not dramatic, ways.

As people do now, Whitelanders ate, slept, made love, raised children, and tried to keep body and soul together by finding ways to make a living. In so doing, they sustained a society, a polity, and an economy, although it would never have occurred to them to use those high-flown academic terms as descriptors of their lives.

They were well informed. They read newspapers, listened to

radio, and, at the cinema, watched *Movietone News*—the movie house precursor of television news. They debated the bright ideas of the New Dealers and felt fear and concern about the turmoil in Europe as nation-states led by tyrants like Hitler, Mussolini, and Stalin mobilized for a World War I rematch. A few Whitelanders were World War I veterans who had had direct involvement in Europe's extreme politics, that is, bloody fighting. Others were young men who would soon have that same experience.

They had opinions, plenty of them. But they were mainly preoccupied with the task of making a living. The following is about their lives, as I observed them firsthand as a youth. It is a collection of sketches mingled with some critical observations about the public policies that came to bear on them.

It is partly a book about economic policy, but never fear. There are no fifty-dollar words or squiggly equations or even graphs. It approaches economics as a behavioral science, if one chooses to believe that the study of human behavior can ever be considered a science.

I came out of that small-town environment to spend a long career as a writer and editor at the *Wall Street Journal* engaged almost daily with the interaction of politics and economics, and it never seemed like much of a science to me. Rather it seemed like an interplay of many millions of humans seeking to fulfill their needs and wants through private transactions. Too often, I think, they sought to reach those objectives through politics, which entails calling forth the coercive power of government.

That is a key point of this book. Governments over the last century or so have expanded under the rubric of what has come to be called "economic policy." In the baldest terms, that means the passage of laws or issuance of binding regulations attempting to guide the behavior of individuals as they go about their daily lives producing goods and services, buying and selling, or investing in the enterprise of other producers.

This governmental masterminding often causes outright damage, as was the case in the 1930s. That's because nobody is smart enough to "manage" a national economy, no matter how many economics Ph.D.s they assemble. An economy, encompassing billions of transactions daily and subject to buffeting from worldwide events like wars and natural disasters, is infinitely complex.

Governments have a natural tendency to grow and expand their power. That, after all, is what governments do: govern. As they reach into more and more areas of human endeavor, the likelihood increases that they will tilt the balance to serve selfish political ends, or simply get things wrong. Today's widespread distrust of government, as indicated by opinion polls, surely reflects a feeling by many Americans that Washington interferes too much and too often gets things wrong.

Modern economists have developed extensive tools for taking the temperature of national and global economies, measuring such things as gross production of goods and services, changes in average prices, or the number of people in the national workforce. But even the accuracy of these tools is constantly debated. Is the Bureau of Labor Statistics' "market basket" used for measuring prices valid, considering the fact that consumer needs and preferences change over time? What does a falling unemployment rate really tell you when so many people who were once considered part of the workforce have given up looking for work?

So, if even the measurements of economic health or malaise are exceedingly difficult to execute, what should we think about government's use of its police powers to actually try to control and direct economic behavior? Quite likely, the broad public is right in treating these efforts with far more skepticism than they usually get from either academia or the press.

The policy prescriptions of academics and coverage of economic news often imply that the president and other makers of economic policy somehow "run" the economy, or more implausibly that the president "runs" the entire country. That would have been a good trick even in 1930, when the country was only one-third as populous as now, which is why the New Deal experiments in central planning, thank heaven, mostly flopped. Today there can be serious doubts that the president even "runs" the government, given the plethora of independent regulatory agencies and empire builders within the federal bureaucracy. But it seems that we again are seeing more constitutional abuses by the executive branch like those of the 1930s and that the Supreme Court is less active than it was then in policing those abuses.

This book harks back to a time when economic planners, of first one party and then the other, were coming into prominence, issuing one sweeping dictum after another and totally mismanaging that vital medium of exchange and measure of value, the U.S. dollar. It was a decade that saw two spectacular stock market crashes and double-digit levels of joblessness.

We will look at all the lever-pulling in Washington, D.C., from the perspective of the people of Whiteland, one of thousands of small farm towns at a time when the economy was heavily agrarian. Farmers had a lot of political power but often didn't know how to use it in their own best interests, simply because they didn't know where their best interests lay.

People described in this book made the best of things and in so doing kept the wheels of a heavily burdened economy turning. They were individuals like Ralph Barger, the dwarf drayman whose handicap didn't prevent him from delivering coal to townspeople, and "Sam" Battin, who built a plumbing business from what he had learned about pipe fitting doing maintenance work at the canning factory.

There were some casualties in terms of lost jobs and lost farms, but for the most part, people coped, preserving the economic infrastructure that their forebears had so laboriously built and even expanding it despite the uncertainties engendered by government experiments. Uncertainties such as these prompted Ronald Reagan, who came of age during the Depression, to utter those oft-quoted words: "In our present crisis, government isn't the solution to our problem, government IS the problem."

Again, economics is about human behavior, which is extremely difficult if not impossible to evaluate and predict "scientifically." A realistic approach recognizes that economies are built from the ground up, not the top down, by the endeavors of individuals to improve their lives through work, imagination, and initiative. That's what the people of Whiteland did because they were fortunate enough to have the freedom to do so.

After mastering hard times, we went into World War II confident of victory, achieved it in large part because of the innovation and productive power of a vibrant capitalist economy, and came out with a new appreciation of our system and with greatly expanded global responsibilities. Victory changed the tenor of the times.

Maybe these glimpses will tell us something about our own era and provide some insight into what is meant by the term "American exceptionalism," mainly why it is more than a chauvinistic boast. A good synonym would be "economic freedom." Those often-used words might sound like a cliché to many modern ears. But people I have met who have suffered under political tyranny, even the soft tyranny of what still remains of the British class system, understand clearly what American "exceptionalism" means. They know the difference freedom makes in the quality of one's life.

Americans by and large have been among the fortunate people of the world. There have been relatively few restrictions on their ability to exercise their natural creativity and profit from their toil. They have made the most of it, building an economic colossus and producing, along with their partners in like-minded nations like postwar Japan, a wonderland of technological marvels.

Does a new, bright generation of Americans, the teachers who instruct them, and the politicians who lead them understand how this greatness came about? Do they understand that the economy is not something "managed" or "grown" by politicians, but is rather the sum total of the work effort and creativity of an entire population? These private efforts are often inhibited by the mistakes of Washington, but if not too heavily burdened they provide the locomotion for greater abundance and higher living standards. Is that understood? Maybe so, maybe not. Hence this book.

CHAPTER ONE

★

WELCOME TO THE VILLAGE

Imagine yourself transported back in time eighty-three years, to April 1933, and deposited in Indianapolis, the capital of Indiana. You've just treated yourself to a room at the Claypool Hotel, which cost $8 plus an outrageous 50 cents for breakfast. But it was worth it. You feel rested as a bellhop loads your suitcase into the rumble seat of your Model A Ford coupe. Feeling generous, you tip him a quarter; he breaks out in a big smile and is your friend for life.

You take a turn around what locals call "the circle" to view the city's centerpiece, the 284-foot-high Soldiers' and Sailors' Monument, dedicated thirty years earlier to the state's war dead, and then you head south on Meridian Street. Since most of the city's 360,000 people live north of the circle, you are out of town in five minutes on a two-lane road that was designated U.S. Highway 31 when the federal highway system was pieced together out of state and local roads a few years earlier. That stretch would soon become a brick road, courtesy of Governor Paul V. McNutt, whose family law firm was sited in Martinsville, one of the state's largest brick producers, and whose home was in Franklin, where the brick would terminate.

Your Ford Model A ping-pings along nicely, making a more advanced sound than the putt-putt of its predecessor, the Model T, mainly because the A was in fact markedly more advanced than the T. It had not only a more powerful engine but a clutch, gearshift, and accelerator pedal replacing the forward and reverse foot pedals and hand throttle of the T. You drive at a safe speed of 35 miles an hour and enjoy the signs of spring. It's a tranquil scene, with farmers plowing their fields behind teams of horses, or in some cases pulling their plows with a Fordson or Farmall tractor. There isn't much traffic.

You pass through the town of Greenwood, population just over 2,300, keeping a sharp lookout for the Interurban railcars that glide down the middle of Madison Avenue. These high-speed trolley cars were a principal mode of transport when autos were in their infancy, hence their pride of place down Greenwood's main artery. Their tracks radiate out from their huge barnlike terminus in Indianapolis like spokes of a wheel to towns throughout the region. This one carries passengers to and fro between Indianapolis and Louisville, Kentucky, stopping at small towns along the way. They flash across

Highway 31 at times, as if the track builders couldn't make up their minds about which side of the highway they wanted to be on. Be sure and heed the flashing signals at the crossings because a collision with an Interurban could spoil your day.

Four miles south of Greenwood, five miles before you reach the Johnson County seat, Franklin, and just after you've passed another Interurban crossing, you see on your right a sign notifying you that you have reached Whiteland, Pop. 406.

The population number is marvelously specific, but that's not to say it is accurate. The 1930 census, surely the count the sign maker was attempting to use, had given Whiteland 13 more souls, listing its population at 419. When the Melloan family would move there late in 1933 from a farm west of town, we would add another 10. So the sign, which stood for many years, merely signified that you were entering a small town, or more accurately driving past most of it.

Indianapolis at that time billed itself as the "Crossroads of America," a slogan that had some legitimacy since two main U.S. highways, 31 and 40, crossed there and most of America's population at that time lay east of the Mississippi River. The mean center of the U.S. population in 1930, as statistically determined by the Census Bureau, is just sixty miles southwest of where you are now, in Linton, Indiana.

You want to find out how the people of a small town in the hinterland are doing at a time when the economy is in a deep economic slump. So you turn left on the concrete Whiteland Road between John Scott's general store and a shiny white Linco service station to drive into what is known as Old Whiteland.

You pass a short side street on your right leading to Jack

McIntire's garage, where Jack and his mechanics are busy giving a 1926 Chevrolet new piston rings and fixing the clutch on a John Deere GP tractor. Then you see the brick Methodist church, cross the small bridge spanning Brewer Ditch, go past the Pleasant Township consolidated school on your left, and are now in downtown Whiteland. On your right, down Pearl Street, you can glimpse the small, white-frame Baptist church.

Downtown is represented by a fire house sheltering an old Ford Model T pumper, then a one-story brick building housing just about everything else you might need: a barbershop, the post office, the small Whiteland restaurant, and John Earhart's grocery store.

Farther on eastward in a small white-frame building is Harry Porter's drugstore and, after that the brick Whiteland National Bank building, currently shuttered. On the right is Shelby Duncan's cobbler shop and the old Thompson Hotel, now converted to small apartments.

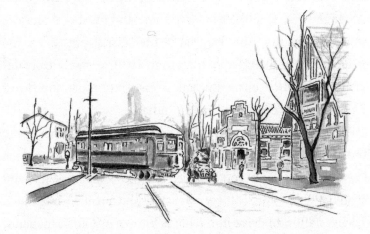

Just before Porter's, Railroad Street branches off to the left and you pass Frank Richardson's blacksmith shop. Farther on the right is the only tall building, the Valentine brothers' grain elevator, with its weigh station and coal yard. Crossing the Pennsylvania Railroad track beyond the elevator, you come upon the county road that leads leftward to the town's only industry, the Stokely Brothers canning factory, and southward past Baughman's general store and the railroad depot, back to Main Street. Flora and Homer Fisher operate a general store on the left corner and across Main Street in a small brick building is the Whiteland telephone exchange. Turn left on Main and after a hundred yards you pass the Presbyterian church on your left. A hundred feet on and you're out of town.

That's pretty much it. Everything looks normal. The townspeople are going about their daily routines, picking up their mail from their boxes at the post office. Whiteland doesn't have home mail delivery. Its streets don't have street signs, so the knowledge of their names is only registered in the memories of townspeople. Houses aren't numbered, but then everyone knows where everyone else lives. Hence, people go to the post office for the mail; it doesn't come to them.

Early birds are shopping for groceries. Pupils and teachers are beginning the school day as five yellow buses deliver the farm kids, who scurry to their classrooms. Frank Richardson is shoeing a horse outside his shop. John Yaste is funneling grain from the elevator by means of a long spout into a railcar on the Pennsylvania Railroad siding. Mailman Johnny Duggan is loading up his Chevy to begin his rural route deliveries.

You might not know that there is a depression on, and
therein lies an anomaly. We look back on the Great Depression today as an economic disaster, and for many Americans
it was. Charitable groups set up soup kitchens in the cities to
feed the hungry jobless. Men snagged onto freight cars for
free rides to places with greater job prospects. These "hobos"
showed up at many a back door in the towns, asking housewives for something to eat, and were almost always obliged.
(Mary Minner in Franklin once had a hobo refuse her offer
of biscuits and gravy; he explained that he didn't like biscuits
and gravy and would go elsewhere to seek a better offering.)
Banks went bust and farms were foreclosed. There were hun-
ger demonstrations in some cities. Congress passed the Federal Emergency Relief Act to funnel money to state, county,
and city relief agencies to help buy food and medicine for the
destitute.

But in the thousands of small towns that dotted the country, life went on. The country did not shut down, either in
an economic or a cultural sense. Indeed, popular culture
flourished. Hollywood made some of its best movies in the
1930s, like *It Happened One Night* (1934) and *Gone with the
Wind* (1939). "Classics" of that era are frequently replayed on
cable channels. Cole Porter was writing tuneful songs with
endearing lyrics, like "You're the Tops" and "Night and Day,"
for the big bands of Tommy Dorsey and Glenn Miller to play
and pretty girls like Jo Stafford and Dinah Shore to sing. Great
black musicians like composer-bandleader Duke Ellington,
singer-trumpeter Louis Armstrong, and such talents as Ella
Fitzgerald and Billie Holiday enriched our lives and lifted the

consciousness of many right-thinking Americans to the evils of racial discrimination.

Despite the richness of life that marked the 1930s, Whitelanders had certainly seen better times. Older farmers had done better in the early part of the century when the dollar was under the stabilizing influence of the international gold standard and global demand for their products was strong. The year 1912 was so good that farmers in the 1930s and thereafter would use farm prices in that year as the benchmark of their demands for "parity," meaning government supports that would restore prices to the 1912 level.

The 1920s had seen a profusion of motorcars and new types of labor-saving electric appliances, like vacuum cleaners and washing machines. Housing starts had boomed. Rising productivity, through greater electrification and mechanization of industry, had created more leisure time and higher living standards. Some New Deal historians would later complain that wage gains didn't match the productivity increases, as an argument that factory workers had been victimized, but it's not clear that a simple comparison of wages and productivity adds up to "unfairness." Investment in capital equipment is a large factor in expanding productivity.

Old John Scott, the Whiteland storekeeper, had shared in the good life of the 1920s, traveling around the populated eastern half of the country with a carnival troupe. He owned a Ferris wheel that he moved, disassembled, by freight car with the other carnival rides and equipment. The troupe played county and state fairs and John and his fellows sometimes set up their rides and booths independently in empty lots or open fields.

Trouping gave him an education in the distinctive regional ethnic customs and mores of a society that in the 1920s had not yet been homogenized by modern forms of transportation and communication. His Ferris wheel furnished joy to the children of Germans in Pennsylvania, Swedes in Minnesota, and Poles in Michigan, many of them recent immigrants from Europe who were melding themselves into an economy and culture more vigorous and promising than the ones they left behind.

The nation's population in 1930 was only 123 million, about one-third what it is today. Almost half lived in rural areas, on farms or in small towns like Whiteland. People of these small communities strongly identified themselves with their own hometowns, which provided them with a strong sense of civic pride, even if their civic achievement was nothing more than installing streetlights on the main drag through town. It was an age when families mostly stayed put, far less true in today's age of greater mobility as people move from town to town, state to state, and even abroad with greater frequency. Whitelanders' contact with the larger world was limited mostly to what they read in newspapers, heard on the radio, or saw in the movies.

Some villagers had seen worse times than the Depression era. Ed Speas had gotten a whiff of mustard gas in the trenches of France in 1918, courtesy of the German army. His son, Jimmy, interrupted our play one day to take me into the house to see a musty relic, the gas mask his father had brought home from World War I. It was a hideous-looking khaki thing, with goggles and an ugly snout that contained the air filter. It invoked the image of soldiers garbed like monsters engaged in combat in the mud and gore. But it may have saved Ed's life. Otherwise, Jimmy wouldn't have been there.

Farmer Roy Sharp had lost his first wife in the great international influenza epidemic of 1918–20, which had afflicted 28 percent of the U.S. population and killed an estimated 500,000–675,000 people. It was a terrible time, with mothers fearing for the lives of their small children, who were especially vulnerable and many of whom were among the victims.

Alcohol prohibition, mandated in 1920 under the Eighteenth Amendment to the Constitution, had claimed victims as well. Innocents sometimes were killed or wounded in the shootings and bombings that were part of bootleg gang warfare in cities like Chicago. Bootleg booze was sometimes poisonous. It was said that for a time Pat Good, the local Stokely factory manager, periodically had to swallow a golf ball–sized silk ball on a string and then retrieve it to keep open an esophagus damaged by too-potent bootleg gin.

One Whiteland townsman, according local legend, had become so desperate for a drink that he sampled wood alcohol, used as a car radiator antifreeze, thereby rendering himself blind. When I saw him walking about the town with his white cane, the only blind man in Whiteland, I wondered whether that story was really true or if someone had just made it up.

In April 1933, the new administration of Franklin Delano Roosevelt was in power. FDR had delivered his famous inaugural address on March 4 in a somber tone, saying the country was in a deep crisis and was hence in need of radical measures to revive the economy, measures that he in fact would design and implement.

Two members of FDR's initial three-member "brain trust" crafting his revolutionary program were men from small towns much like Whiteland. Raymond Moley was from Berea, Ohio, and Rexford Tugwell was from a farm village called Sinclairville, in western New York State. The two economists were recruited from the faculty of that distinguished New York Ivy League school, Columbia University. The third member, Adolf Berle, was a Boston-born New York lawyer. They would have an important role in designing the truckload of legislation that moved through Congress in FDR's first one hundred days, with Tugwell focusing on the restrictive farm legislation that soon would change the traditional ways of Whiteland-area farmers.

The people of Whiteland were aware of all the excitement in Washington and to some it sounded good that the president had hired certifiably bright men to help him solve the nation's problems. They had yet to see how all that would turn out, particularly the farm measures designed by Tugwell, an ardent believer in government economic planning.

But meanwhile, Whitelanders were dealing with the realities of life, not the abstractions of economic revolution. They were growing crops, repairing cars and tractors, digging holes and ditches for the septic tanks needed for indoor plumbing, warehousing cases of canned tomatoes at the canning factory, and providing to their fellow men and women whatever other goods or services were marketable. My cousin Dorothy McClain had an in-home beauty parlor where local women could pay a few dollars for permanent waves to make themselves more fetching and boost their morale. The sturdy Gertrude Lewis performed that task economists often refer to as a fundamental example of human commerce. She took in other people's laundry.

Their work efforts and those of others like them were the substance of the economy that the theorists in Washington were trying to micromanage through legislation or, in the case of the Federal Reserve Board, the ineffectual manipulation of bank interest rates to serve any number of contradictory purposes, such as maintaining what little was left of the gold standard while at the same time providing an adequate money supply. Washington micromanagement wasn't faring well, but Whiteland's villagers soldiered on because they had to, trying to shrug off the government policy mistakes that had created an unstable currency and a sharp reduction in agricultural trade, both of which were damaging to the incomes of people in farm communities.

In the end, the people prevailed. The work effort and ingenuity of ordinary people, like the Whitelanders, in America's towns and cities sustained the economy through a rough decade, keeping alive the latent dynamism that delivered to Americans the high standard of living and the technological wonders that we enjoy today.

It was in the 1930s that I grew from childhood to puberty in Whiteland. Interestingly enough, I, along with many of my contemporaries, remember our childhoods in this era of too little money and economic uncertainty as a happy time. Indeed, in 2002 my late friend Hugh Jackson Ross self-published a charming collection of his fond memories and those of our fellow townspeople, a book I will quote from time to time. An examination of our experiences, and of how the people of Whiteland survived an excess of experimentation by their elected federal officials, may offer clues about why the nation proved so resilient in dealing with the Depression and the world war that followed.

CHAPTER TWO

THE FAMILY ODYSSEY

James and Sara Ollie

Yᴏᴜʀ ᴛᴏᴜʀ ᴏꜰ the town precedes by a few months the date when the Melloan family first fetched up there. Like several Whiteland families, ours came to Indiana from Kentucky, or at least eight of the ten of us did. One of the natural migratory routes in pioneer times led from Virginia through the Cumberland Gap into Kentucky and then on north. Another natural route was down the Ohio River from Fort Pitt (now Pittsburgh) to the various jumping-off towns in southern Indiana or northern Kentucky.

But we didn't talk much about our Kentucky origins. Kentucky's mountainous east was a poor area and its many untutored "hillbillies" came north in summer to find work in the fields and canning factories. These were mostly hardworking, decent people, but native Hoosiers tended to look down on them and Kentuckians in general. So we didn't advertise our Kentucky heritage, rich as it might have been. Neither did some of our fellow townspeople with the same history. For years, I didn't know about the Kentucky background of some of my classmates, because they chose not to tell me. I chose not to tell them about mine, as well. We wanted to assimilate. A mutual suspicion between the two states still exists, manifesting itself particularly when the University of Kentucky Wildcats and Indiana University Hoosiers battle each other on the basketball courts.

Whitelanders were mostly white Protestants with Anglican, German, or Dutch names and bloodlines that traced back to Europe. Some families, like mine, also had ancestors that sprang from the forests of the aboriginal American continent. My mother used to joke that her people didn't come over on the *Mayflower,* they were here to meet the boat. It was not entirely a joke; her great-great-grandmother was Cherokee.

James Melloan and Sara Ollie Meredith grew up on farms near Horse Cave, Kentucky, fell in love, and were married in Munfordville, the Hart County seat, on December 4, 1904. Their fathers had both fought on the Union side in the Civil War, with Abraham Meredith having seen action in the famous "battle above the clouds" on Lookout Mountain in northern Tennessee. James William Melloan was a member of the 21st Kentucky Volunteer Infantry, which participated in fourteen battles, the most of any Kentucky fighting unit. Each attained the rank of corporal.

Sara had been orphaned at age fourteen when Abraham was the victim of a freak accident. He was riding home on his horse past a sawmill when the mill's boiler exploded, apparently because the attendant had gone to sleep and failed to monitor the boiler's pressure level. Abraham was knocked off his horse by a large piece of steel and died instantly. Sara, whose mother had died earlier, went to live with Pernia, a married older sister in nearby Scottsville.

James and Sara had some colorful ancestors. Sara's great-great-grandfather was a French fur trader named Timothy Demonbreun, who had come down the river system from Quebec in the late eighteenth century to set up a post to buy pelts from Indian trappers on the site of what is now Nashville, Tennessee. Nashvillians today honor him with a statue and street named for him in "Music City." According to some records, he sired two families: one in Kaskaskia, Illinois, with a French wife and the other in Nashville, the product of his liaison with a Cherokee woman who in subsequent records would bear a French name, Elizabeth Durard. She was the great-great-grandmother my mother referred to. Life on the frontier was not always conducted by the rules of established society.

We learn from research by the Timothy Demonbreun Society of Nashville that Timothy got his strange name from one of his paternal ancestors, Pierre Boucher, who had migrated as a thirteen-year-old with his family to Quebec from

Mortagne in the French province of Perche in 1635. His father, Gaspard, was one of the first white settlers of the North American continent. Young Pierre became a protégé of the Jesuit fathers who had first explored that area; he learned the Huron Indian language and served as an interpreter. As an adult he became a leader of the French settlement of Trois-Rivières, Quebec, organizing a successful defense against attacks by the Iroquois, who were hostile to both the Hurons and the French. As a reward, the French crown in Paris gave him a noble title and the right to bestow titles on his fifteen sons. The colony sent him back to France to plead with Louis XIV for crown recognition of New France and the dispatch of troops for its defense.

He was popular in France particularly because he had authored a booklet describing the beauties of Quebec in terms a Madison Avenue copywriter would admire, noting that the wild blackberries were larger than the berries cultivated in France and that the lakes and forests were teeming with fish and game. The main question he was asked by Frenchmen: Can you make money there? He answered yes. He got his troops and protection from the French crown for New France. No doubt by giving Pierre and his sons titles, Louis had in mind creating for New France an aristocracy beholden to the crown. It didn't work out quite that way.

One of Pierre's sons received the title of Sieur [Lord] Étienne Boucher de Mont Brun (Brown Mountain). Generations later, Timothy found his inherited title cumbersome and meaningless in the wilderness. Native Americans and in fact Americans in general weren't much impressed with French titles. They were far more impressed by Timothy's martial abilities. He helped General George Rogers Clark hold the Mississippi River territories during the American Revolution. Sieur Jacques-Timothé Boucher de Montbrun was known to one and all as Timothy Demonbreun.

As for my father, his surname came from John Smith Melloan, born in County Tyrone, Ireland, who washed ashore at Maysville, Kentucky, early in 1825 or thereabouts. The story was that he and a brother were traveling down the Ohio River from Pittsburgh on a flatboat when a fight broke out on deck and the brother was thrown overboard. John jumped in to save him but was a poor swimmer, as was his brother, and they couldn't fight the river current. The brother drowned; John made it to shore.

The young Irishman, having arrived in Maysville in such a damp and distressed condition, stayed on. He courted and married Lydia Houghton, whose father had migrated to Maysville through the Cumberland Gap from Hopewell, New Jersey. Her grandfather, Joab Houghton, was commemorated by a plaque on a stone in Hopewell for having stood there and shouted to the menfolk of town one Sunday after church: "The Redcoats are murdering our brethren in Massachusetts. Who will go with me to fight?" Every man stepped forward, says the plaque, although it doesn't record whether they actually went. Joab, however, did become a lieutenant colonel in Washington's army and did in fact fight the Redcoats.

Some years ago, my sister Marie and I visited his still-standing stone house, now marked as a historic site. The present owners who invited us to come in and look around

were a nice British couple, perhaps descended from those
Redcoats who once came searching that same house for Joab.
Reconciliation at last.

After their marriage, John S. and Lydia Melloan did what
many young couples did in the early nineteenth century. They
headed farther west—but not very far. They found a large
parcel of fairly decent farming land in the cave country of
central Kentucky, some of which is now part of Mammoth
Cave National Park. The nearest town was Horse Cave, which
has a cave in the middle of town so named, according to one
legend, because an unfortunate horse had once tumbled into
the deep hole that formed the entrance.

Having married in Munfordville, James and Sara stayed in
Hart County long enough to produce a child, Melba Victoria
(Meb) in 1906, but then were taken with the same wander-
lust that had motivated their ancestors. They knew that the
soil was richer north of the Ohio River on the alluvial plain
formed eons ago by ice-age glaciers. They learned of a sharecropping opportunity near Monmouth, Illinois, packed their
meager belongings, bundled up baby Meb, and caught a train
north.

Conrad Barry (Connie) and William Thomas (Bill) were
added to the family in Illinois. After five years in Illinois, and
a brief sojourn on a farm in Iowa, James and Sara had saved
enough money for a down payment on a farm of their own
and through their Kentucky relatives found a 120-acre spread
on the eastern outskirts of Louisville.

The only problem was that the farm was bordered on the
north by the mighty Ohio River, which overflowed its banks

every spring. That was bad and good. When the Ohio flooded, the Melloans had to move their children, belongings, and team of horses to temporary quarters on a bluff above the farm. And when the flood subsided Dad had to clear his land of debris, mainly tree stumps and limbs, using his horses and chains to drag the heavy items off the land.

Their main house was on stilts but even so they had to dry it out as well. It was primitive living. Connie remembers coming down the stairs one morning and seeing a copperhead snake lying at the foot of the steps. Copperheads were poisonous and, dangerous because they were brown and blended with the soil and, unlike rattlers, made no noise. But they smelled like cucumbers, so if you smelled cucumbers you knew that there was either a copperhead or a cucumber patch nearby. It was a good idea to find out which. Connie remembered that Dad's technique for killing snakes was to pick them up by the tail and snap them like a whip.

Connie contracted malaria. Mom always blamed that for his small size, about five foot five and 130 pounds. Mosquitoes, flies, gnats, and other insects were constant companions in summer. Bill, two years younger, once scoffed at that theory: "Hell, we all had malaria."

The good side was that the flooded Ohio brought a fresh deposit of rich topsoil that had once belonged to farmers to the east in Ohio and Pennsylvania. As soon as Dad's land was dry enough, he planted sweet corn. When the roasting ears were mature and succulent, he broke them off their stalks, piled them into his farm wagon, and hauled them into the Louisville market to sell to townspeople.

It was a good business. On the return trip late at night, Dad kept a pearl-handled Smith & Wesson revolver beside him on the wagon seat to ward off Louisville thugs who might be tempted to rob him of his day's takings. No attempt was ever made, perhaps because the word had gone around the Louisville underworld that he was armed.

The Melloans lived on that farm for seven years, during which three more children, Lillian Lorraine (Sis), Charles Robert (Bob), and James Patrick (Jim), were born. The oldest three, Meb, Connie, and Bill, caught a trolley car near their house and rode eastward to Prospect, Kentucky, to attend the Ballard School. Sis always longed to join them but she was too young. I took her to visit the Ballard School in 1988 and she was thrilled to finally see the place she had dreamed about as a child but had never before seen.

The Melloans did well enough in Kentucky that in late 1917, when word came from Mom's older brother Bert of a new opportunity in Indiana, they had enough money to move on. Bert had migrated to Indiana years earlier as a farmhand and had married the farmer's only child—thus marrying a farm, so to speak. Bert wrote that there was a good sixty-acre farm for sale west of Greenwood. He put Dad in touch with his friend Charlie Durham, also a Kentuckian (from Bowling Green) and now cashier of the Whiteland National Bank.

The sale was managed and in January 1918, Dad put Sara Ollie and their six children on a train for Indiana. He rode with them across the Ohio River, apparently out of a concern about that great and treacherous barrier. His concerns would have been heightened by the fact that the train stopped on the bridge for two hours, leaving them wondering what had gone wrong. But when it was finally across he hopped off and returned to the farm to manage its sale.

That was a milestone year for the family but not a good year for the country. American boys were fighting in Europe. An influenza pandemic would soon be ravaging the United States and the world at large. It was bitter cold, there was deep snow, and the train crept along for eight hours to cover the hundred miles to Whiteland. There was not much heat in their coach. A kindly woman from Indianapolis held baby Jim. Five-year-old Lorraine threw up. Mom wiped it up with one of Jim's diapers and tossed it out the train window, wondering if there was any law against tossing diapers out of train windows. Twelve-year-old Melba, already becoming a second mother, helped look after the younger ones.

Uncle Bert and his father-in-law, Jasper "Jap" Shutters, met them at the Whiteland depot, both driving one-horse sleighs. The Melloans were bundled up and taken to Bert's farm, three miles west of Whiteland. Bert's wife, Aunt Met, greeted them from the doorway, silhouetted by the lamplight behind her. After that awful trip, "she looked like an angel," Sis recalled. "She was a saint."

The Melloans did well on the farm west of Greenwood. They bought a car, a big black 1922 Chalmers touring car, with a canvas top and glassine side curtains to keep out the rain and snow, suitable for transporting a big family. The Chalmers had problems with the design of the rear differential joint so that it made a grinding sound when you rounded a turn. James and Sara eventually traded it for a Model T. Superior engineering explains why Ford, but not Chalmers, is still a household name. They were able to afford a pony for Connie and a piano for music lessons for the kids.

Marie was born in March 1925. Melba, bright and pretty, graduated from Greenwood High School that same year and became a bookkeeper for a thriving Chevrolet dealership, Kelly Sales Company. Connie graduated three years later and found work as an auto mechanic.

But alas, things took a nasty turn for the worse in the summer of 1926. Dad had become involved with Uncle Bert and banker Durham in cattle trading. He signed the 1926 equivalent of a cattle futures contract that Charlie's bank was offering, betting on a rise in cattle prices from the early 1926 level of $11.11 a hundredweight. Instead, prices dropped to $9.98 by midyear when his contract came due. It was out of the money and he couldn't sell it. So instead of cash, he got the animals themselves.

Trucks from southern Indiana pulled up and loaded bulls

into his barnyard. Bedlam ensued. It was a terrible scene, a barnyard full of bawling hungry, thirsty, and dangerous animals. Dad eventually managed to get them loaded up and hauled off to the stockyard, but he took a huge loss, equivalent to about $70,000 today. Eventually, he couldn't afford payments on the Whiteland Bank mortgage so after the summer of 1927 we lost the farm. As Connie put it later, "Dad wasn't smart enough to do business with those two birds," meaning Bert, a canny trader, and Charlie, a professional moneyman. "So we became sharecroppers again."

Connie was being a bit unfair. Dad was no dummy, or he couldn't have come as far as he did. But he was a straight arrow who didn't smoke, drink, or swear. And even after a long career in the farming business, he was still a bit naïve. Wives of men whose mistakes threaten the security of the family do not take such things lightly. Said Sara Melloan: "I always told James not to trust those Merediths." She was referring to her brother, Bert.

My arrival in the world was not particularly opportune for our family, since we had just lost the farm. We were wintering in a little frame house alongside the main street of Greenwood, Madison Avenue, waiting to move to another farm where we would indeed once again be sharecroppers.

But my parents, although shocked by our loss, didn't regard me as an added burden, nor did my now three sisters and four brothers. Farm families of that era didn't regard new arrivals as another mouth to feed, but as additional contributions of human capital to spread the hard work of farming that involved horse-drawn plows, hand milking, tub laundering, and home canning, to cite a few examples. Even as sharecroppers, and even in the hard times that were coming, every available hand was valuable. An extra mouth to feed was of little consequence on a farm where what we needed we could grow ourselves.

It's interesting that farm families were more advanced in their thinking about human resources than some of our national policy makers, then and today. Herbert Hoover banned immigration during the deepening recession and some Republicans today are equally paranoid about immigrants. But the more enlightened view, or so I believe, is that human beings on average produce more than they consume. Thus, given good free-market economic policies, immigrants will expand output and economic growth for themselves, the community, and the nation.

An example is the West German *wirtschaftswunder*, or post–World War II "economic miracle," widely attributed to the large flight of able-bodied Germans to the capitalist West from the communist East at a time when the West's economics minister, Ludwig Erhard, was liberalizing the West German economy along free-market lines. That success supported the argument that humans should be properly recognized as a resource, not a burden. Such a belief was instinctive to farmers. That's why so many farm couples had large families. And maybe I owe my own existence to that principle, because I was the last of the eight children James and Ollie produced.

CHAPTER THREE

★

WHAT CRASH?

I WAS A TODDLER approaching my second birthday on what was called "the old Davis place" west of Whiteland, which we were sharecropping, on October 24, 1929, when prices on the New York Stock Exchange took a nosedive, leaving banks and investors with holdings a lot less valuable than the day before. Unsurprisingly, the crash was of little concern to me. But then it also wasn't of much concern to the editors of our county seat newspaper, the *Franklin Evening Star*. They didn't bother to report it, according to a recent microfiche search at the Franklin Public Library by my childhood friend, Carolyn Wendt of Whiteland.

Maybe that made sense. Few if any people in Johnson County owned New York–listed common stocks or securities of any kind, for that matter. New York was a long way away in 1929 in terms of the time and money needed to get there, and what happened in the Big Apple, unless it was something like the 1927 celebration of Charles Lindbergh's first solo flight across the Atlantic, was of little concern to the *Star*'s editors.

They were mistaken about the crash, of course, but had no way of knowing it at the time. The well-trusted Herbert Hoover was president with a Republican Congress friendly toward farmers and business. What could go wrong? The *Star*'s editors and all the rest of us would soon find out.

One might say that President Hoover's problem was that he was *too* friendly toward farmers and business and too eager to use the tools of government to try to bail them out of difficulties they should have resolved on their own. The brainy engineer, who had become a hero in Europe when he organized World War I food relief, had won widespread popular acclaim when he led his Republican Party to a victory in the national elections of 1928. But what with one thing and another, the 1929 stock market crash included, things had not gone well.

The federal government wasn't very big at that time. In 1930, federal tax receipts consumed only 4.8 percent of the nation's gross national product (GNP), compared with about 18 percent today. Yet during the Hoover era Washington became more activist, seeking to manage economic forces through government intervention. As Americans have recently been reminded, the failures of intervention often lead not to less of it, but more. Hoover's policy failures brought on a new regime, the New Deal. led by Franklin D. Roosevelt, and government intervention into the economy to levels never seen before. We are still witnessing some of the consequences, such as a continuing government support for, and supervision of, the farming industry.

As an inevitable result of these interventions, businesses, and farmers in particular, were less free to adapt to changing costs of their inputs and the prices they could get for their outputs. In a free market, the normal response to falling prices would be to redirect resources—capital, land, and labor—into more profitable ventures. This process of adaptation preserves what economists call "economic efficiency." The more efficient an economy, the more likely it is to expand and yield greater prosperity to the people who create it.

Sadie Henry in Whiteland knew all that instinctively. The more rapidly and efficiently she and her husband, Ray, could hang wallpaper, the more customers they could satisfy and the more money they would make. If demand for wallpapering was slack, they could switch to painting or some other useful service. She and Ray would have been far less efficient if some government agency had provided them with a subsidy on condition that they stick exclusively to paperhanging. Moreover, their fellow taxpayers would be in the position of supporting their inefficiency.

CHAPTER FOUR

★

THE FARM LOBBY

IN THE 1920S, farming wasn't just any business. According to the 1920 census, people living on farms or in rural towns serving the farm community comprised 48.8 percent of the American population. Farmers not only had influence with their local congressmen; they were also well represented by lobbyists in Washington. The Farm Bureau, the National Farmers Union, co-ops, and the like constituted a powerful political pressure group.

Calvin Coolidge, president from 1923 to 1929, had resisted farm lobby pressures rather effectively, as his biographer Amity Shlaes has noted. He believed that government should wield a light touch in policies impinging on how commodity markets work, or for that matter, on any kind of market. In response to the farm lobbyists' entreaties, he dissembled, observing that farmers had always had trouble making money and saying there wasn't much he could do about it. He once dryly suggested to a farm group lobbying for taxpayer support that taking up religion might serve them better, so one account says.

Years later I would gain firsthand knowledge of the power of the farm lobby, firsthand in a literal sense. When I was about eight or nine, I was often assigned to color the oleo. Oleomargarine was sold in pound cakes that were white. In the package was a packet of orange food coloring. To give oleo the appearance of butter, it was necessary to mix the food coloring with the oleo to produce the yellow that would make it look like butter. I would first wash my hands and then squish the food dye and oleo together to turn it yellow. The food dye colored my hands as well so that after the job was done they were orange. It didn't wash off readily. Orange hands are embarrassing.

I learned that the reason for my embarrassment was a law passed on behalf of the dairy industry to try to fight off competition from the cheaper, vegetable oil–based oleo. Butter prices were artificially elevated by federal price supports called milk marketing orders. So instead of dyeing their oleo at the factory, the oleo makers had to offer the consumer the dye separately. My parents were sympathetic toward the dairy farmers, but they bought oleo nonetheless. And they had me to do the coloring, so it was win-win.

Hoover and the Republican Congress of 1929 were more

sympathetic to farmers than Coolidge had been. They forked
up half a billion dollars to refinance the Farm Loan Board, set
up by the Federal Farm Loan Act (FFLA) of 1916, which supported twelve regional Federal Land Banks. These government-
sponsored banks made preferential loans to farmers, allowing
them to borrow up to 50 percent of the value of their land
on terms of up to forty years. The law specified that interest
could be no more than 6 percent, which meant that they could
borrow from the government at lower rates than from a bank
and for far longer terms.

The problem with the FFLA was that it disadvantaged
privately owned country banks and encouraged farmers to
overborrow and produce more. That created market surpluses
that lowered the value of their crops and were thus self-
defeating. The lobbies blamed the high surpluses of the 1920s
on the recovery of European agriculture from the ravages of
World War I, but they chose not to blame the subsidized lending they had fought for.

Farmer frustration with the surplus-induced low returns
on their crops would lead to the far more serious unintended
consequences of raising protective tariffs. American farmers,
including those around Whiteland who were members of the
Farm Bureau, played a large role in bringing about their own
undoing. To paraphrase an old saying: Be careful what you
lobby for.

CHAPTER FIVE

★

ECONOMIC STUPIDITY

In a speech to the American Bankers Association in October 1930, one year after the crash, President Hoover assured the nation that everything was under control, thanks to his skill in manipulating the levers of government. "I determined that it was my duty, even without precedent, to call upon the business of the country for coordinated and constructive action to resist the forces of disintegration. The business community, the bankers, labor, and the government have cooperated in wider spread measures of mitigation than have ever been attempted before. Our bankers and the reserve system have carried the country through the credit . . . storm without impairment.

Our leading business concerns have sustained wages, have distributed employment, have expedited heavy construction. The Government has expanded public works, assisted in credit to agriculture, and has restricted immigration. These measures have maintained a higher degree of consumption than would otherwise have been the case. They have thus prevented a large measure of unemployment. . . . Our present experience in relief should form the basis of even more amplified plans in the future."

That all sounded good, but as the Mises Institute has argued in its analysis of the Hoover actions, the White House conferences pulling together the combined might of business, labor, and government to maintain employment and wage rates at a time of monetary deflation was probably the worst thing the president could have done. It delayed the market processes through which wages and production would have normally adapted to the reduced consumer demand and falling prices that followed the crash. No such interference had been engineered after the crash of 1920–21 and the economy had quickly recovered.

Corporate chieftains like Gerard Swope of General Electric and Henry Ford accepted it as their patriotic duty to heed the president's request and maintain wage levels in the face of falling prices. William Green, leader of the American Federation of Labor, was certainly on board for this. But of course this patriotic effort organized by the president meant that as prices went down as a result of an unintentional and unmitigated deflationary monetary policy, labor costs stayed up artificially,

rather than adapting to falling prices, weakened banking services, and slowing business activity.

The result was industrial layoffs or in many cases spread-
ing the reduced labor demand by switching full-time workers
to part-time. U.S. Steel went from 225,000 full-time workers
in 1928 to none in 1932—everyone by then was part-time.
This was one of Herbert Hoover's many brushes with the law
of unintended consequences but it hardly deterred him from
further efforts to overpower markets.

He was particularly inept at dealing with the powerful
protectionist forces set in motion by the crash. He initially
opposed the Tariff Act of 1930, coauthored by Senator Reed
Smoot of Utah and Representative Willis C. Hawley of Ore-
gon. It was originally intended as yet another sop for the farm
lobby and probably wouldn't have caused so much trouble
if Congress had known where to stop. America was not a
big importer of farm products, so if they had limited their
bill to tariffs on farm goods, the retaliation from our trading
partners would probably have been fairly light. The United
States had had high tariffs stretching back into the nineteenth
century and indeed they were once the principal source of
government funds. The world trading system had adjusted to
this reality.

But after the 1929 crash, protectionist demands from other
lobbies, including corporations and organized labor, came
pouring in. Republicans did little to resist these importunities
and when the bill was passed in 1930 it was massive. It raised
tariffs on twenty thousand imported items to record levels.

The average ad valorem tariff rate on dutiable goods was set to rise to 50 percent by 1933, or almost double previous levels, already plenty high.

The United States had thrown up a high tariff wall at just the wrong time, after a market crash that had disrupted credit markets globally and made it difficult for would-be importers of American goods to obtain credit. On top of that came the high tariff barrier to reduce their ability to earn dollars with which to buy U.S. goods. Their governments, affronted by the U.S. move, further complicated things by retaliating with higher tariffs of their own, shutting out American exports into European and Asian markets.

After Smoot-Hawley, the 1930 tariff act, U.S. exports nosedived to $1.7 billion in 1933, down from $5.2 billion in 1929. Prices of exportable goods dropped by a third because of reduced foreign demand. Farmers' share of the $3.5 billion in lost American export sales was more than $1 billion. A billion dollars doesn't sound like much today but it was massive in the early 1930s. Total government spending—federal, state, and local—was only $11.9 billion. The loss of export sales, along with a worldwide money shortage (deflation), contributed heavily to the slump in commodity prices that so bedeviled farmers in the early 1930s. Whiteland's farmers would wear their belts tighter as a result.

More than one thousand of the nation's leading economists signed a petition imploring President Hoover not to sign Smoot-Hawley. Henry Ford called it "economic stupidity" and J. P. Morgan CEO Thomas Lamont described it as an "asinine" bill. FDR was against it.

Hoover's emotions may have affected his judgment. He harbored a certain animus toward the Europeans, claiming in speeches that they were guilty of unfair trade and monetary policies. (Does that sound familiar today?) Perhaps his distrust resulted in part from what he had witnessed during World War I, when European leaders had been at their destructive worst. He thus ignored the good advice he was getting. Signing Smoot-Hawley probably did as much as anything to destroy his reputation for wisdom. The Republican Party deservedly lost control of Congress and, with the resounding Democratic election victory of 1932, the door was opened to even greater efforts to manipulate the economy with the advent of the New Deal.

New Dealers would name the shantytowns of the unemployed in the 1930s "Hoovervilles" and would blacken Hoover's name for decades. But instead of learning a lesson from his failures, they would carry on in the same tradition of manic intervention that he initiated when he took office in 1929. Indeed, many of their programs after their sweep, such as heavy public works spending, were built on foundations laid by the Hoover administration.

Smoot-Hawley wasn't the only burden piled on the economy by the Republicans. Gene Smiley, a professor of economics at Marquette University, noted in his 2002 book, *Rethinking the Great Depression,* that the Republicans also raised personal taxes, including the income taxes that higher earners were by then paying. (That sounds a bit familiar today as well.)

"The revenue act of 1932, enacted because of administration and congressional concern over falling government revenues, doubled personal income tax rates," writes Smiley. "The top marginal rate, on income above $750,000, was increased to 63 percent from 25 percent. A wide range of excise taxes was enacted, on everything from gasoline, to electric energy to movie tickets."

That high marginal tax rate on the wealthy might not sound like much, since so few would pay it. But private wealth is the source of capital investment, so taxing the wealthy at a time when a crash has already damaged investor confidence is not the greatest idea in the world. Of course, the excise taxes fell on the nonwealthy and that isn't such a great idea, either, when disposable income already is falling.

The incoming Democrats also had tax ideas. An article in the *Greenwood News* in 1933 told readers that a new 3 percent tax on electricity would cost Public Service Company of Indiana $1,250,000. Under the usual rate setting regulations, most of that cost would be passed along to consumers. The very last thing Hoosiers needed in 1933 was an increase in their light bills. Why Congress chose to tax electricity during a slump is a bit hard to fathom although it may have had to do with the left's political campaign against private utilities and in favor of public power projects like the Tennessee Valley Authority. That fight would last for years.

The Mises Institute study sheds further light on how a rising tax burden, including increases in state and local taxes, afflicted economic growth. It notes that in 1929, the U.S. GNP, or total productive output, was $104.4 billion, of which the private sector accounted for $99.3 billion. Federal tax receipts totaled $5.2 billion and state and local taxes added another

$8.8 billion, for a total of $14 billion. By 1930, GNP had fallen to $91.1 billion, of which $85.8 billion was privately generated. But government receipts dropped by only $500 million. So the burden of government on the economy had grown to 14.8 percent from 13.4 percent. "The fiscal burden of government had substantially increased when it should have been lowered," said the study.

Modern economists who profess to follow the teachings of John Maynard Keynes might say that government did exactly the right thing by raising the tax burden to finance massive expenditures on public works to "stimulate" the economy and provide jobs. The same theory has been applied repeatedly over time, the latest being the massive $871 billion 2009 "stimulus" spending, with hardly sensational results.

Keynes believed that government could ameliorate business cycles through heavy spending during the down cycle. The problem is that to spend, the government has to either tax or borrow, and tax it did in 1930. Hoover spent heavily on public works, including the huge Hoover Dam project, but that didn't prevent the economy from slipping deeper into the depths of depression in 1932.

James Grant, who publishes a savvy securities market newsletter, in 2014 penned a book titled *The Forgotten Depression: 1921: The Crash That Cured Itself,* in which he pointed out that the post–World War I inflation and subsequent slump was a shock arguably as bad as the one in 1929–30. Washington did very little, in contrast with the multiple interventions after the 1929 crash, and a short while later the economy was humming again. Grant makes a persuasive case.

There were astute observers making a similar case eighty-five years ago at the outset of the Great Depression. Albert H. Wiggin, chairman of Chase National Bank, wrote in his January 1931 annual report that production in the preceding year had declined far more than consumption, so it was a fall-off in production, not a lack of "purchasing power," that was causing the slump. As Grant would observe years later, Wiggin noted that during the 1921 depression the lack of government intervention had resulted in costs and wages being quickly scaled down, and unsound activities liquidated. Goods were sold for whatever the market would pay, regardless of what they cost to produce. Some modern economists challenge this "liquidationist" theory, but some of their own ideas have not produced better results.

CHAPTER SIX

MONEY FUMBLES

Folks in whiteland in April 1933 didn't know much about Federal Reserve monetary policy and how it affected the prices of goods they bought and sold. They knew that the paper bills they were using as money were now notes issued

by a Federal Reserve Bank, whereas in the old days, before
the Fed was created in 1913, they might be using notes issued
by their own local banks, backed by the gold they professed
to own. The Whiteland National Bank and the First National
Bank of Greenwood issued such notes, for example.

At the outset of 1933, Americans assumed—because they
had that assurance from the government—that the Federal
Reserve–issued paper dollars in their wallets were backed
by gold in a repository at Fort Knox, Kentucky. To a certain
degree they were right, but the international gold standard at
that point was a shattered remnant of what it once had been
and would soon be abandoned altogether by FDR in a repu-
diation of the use of gold as legal tender. Gold would still be
used in international transactions among central banks.

But if the people of Whiteland didn't understand the in-
tricacies of Federal Reserve money creation, they had a good
excuse. The people who were supposed to be managing the
money supply, including Federal Reserve chairman Eugene
Meyer, a former chemical company executive who took over
in 1930, were having trouble as well. Indeed, it would have
been a miracle if the provably talented Fed chairman had
been able to stabilize the dollar, considering all the economic
variables he was trying to juggle in a new era in which the
set monetary standard of yesteryear, the gold standard, had
become shaky. In 1933, no doubt encouraged by the change of
administration, Meyer gave up tilting at monetary windmills
and took on a more manageable task, running a newspaper.
He bought the distressed *Washington Post*.

Leading monetary economists, ranging from the late Milton Friedman to recent Federal Reserve chairman Ben Bernanke, debated for years the role the Federal Reserve system played in bringing about and prolonging the Great Depression. The only thing most agree upon is that, aside from President Hoover's and FDR's counterproductive governmental interventions in the market, the Fed played a significant role in the 1930s debacle. Some modern economists even argue that the Fed should never have been invented.

In 1928, assuming that the stock boom was a sign of inflation and concerned about the outflow of gold from the United States to England, the Fed began to raise the interest rate on borrowings by commercial banks from Federal Reserve banks, the so-called discount rate. The rate first went to 4 percent from 3.5 percent and then to 5 percent. This had the effect of causing the commercial banks to raise their own short-term interest rates. In early 1929, the Fed's Open Market Committee, dominated by governors appointed by the president, took the additional money-tightening step of selling securities into the market to soak up dollars.

These moves by the Fed dampened the use of bank credit and, according to prevailing theories, aggravated other negative economic factors, including a sharp decline in home building from a robust 1925 peak. Higher borrowing costs and a slowing economy began to let the air out of the stock market. When stocks crashed in October, the loss of liquidity by banks and traders further diminished the money available for business transactions and weakened public confidence in the economy, thus reducing the willingness of consumers to spend. When too much money is chasing too few goods, you get inflation, as reflected by a general rise in prices. But when too little money is chasing too many goods, you get the opposite, a general drop in prices, better known as deflation.

Prices did in fact drop, by more than 23 percent between 1929 and 1933, a big dose of deflation. This is the basis of the argument that the Fed touched off the deflation that bedeviled the Hoover administration and goods and commodity producers—like the Whiteland farmers, for example—during the early 1930s, sometimes called it the "first depression". The Fed would also get a big share of the blame for the "second depression," which started with another market crash in 1937 and continued until war mobilization relieved unemployment in a not very positive way.

Although Meyer opened the monetary spigots when he took over the Fed in 1930, it is argued that he prolonged the deflation by tightening money in 1931, again because of unwarranted fear—so say his critics—of a loss of gold. Mitsubishi Securities economist Brendan Brown argues this point in his 2013 book, *The Global Curse of the Federal Reserve*: "When Britain left the gold standard in September 1931, the Federal Reserve responded to a drain of gold (as investors sought safety from a possible break of the dollar with gold) by raising interest rates sharply, even though there was no immediate lack of 'free gold.'" The Fed action prolonged deflation, he believes. His argument sounds plausible.

Economists usually agree that the international gold standard, which had maintained a reasonable degree of monetary stability through the late 1800s and early 1900s, was fractured by the enormous debts and wastage run up by the European powers in World War I as they fought their bloody and mindless battles, highly costly in money and lives. To finance the war, gold and IOUs flowed to the United States in return for arms, munitions, and supplies.

Under the gold standard, the process usually worked this way: Physical gold was shipped from, say, England to a bank in the United States, which shipped it to a Federal Reserve Bank and had the fixed-rate dollar value, $20.67 an ounce, credited to the bank's reserve account. Postwar gold imports were inflationary, because they expanded the U.S. money supply. Thus, the United States suffered a stiff bout of inflation in the late 1910s, followed by a bust in 1920–21 of about the same magnitude as the one that would come in 1929. Stocks crashed in 1920–21 just as they did in 1929.

But there was a sharp difference between 1921–22 and 1929–30. In the earlier instance the Fed supplied enough liquidity to commercial banks to keep them going, which is what it was originally designed to do during a crisis. From 1929 to 1933, that was not the case. Either because bank failures were too numerous or Fed governors were confused, the Fed was mainly a bystander.

The dislocations of the war years made the Fed's decisions a more crucial factor in how the real economy functioned. Under the international gold standard, monetary policy was set on autopilot, more or less, with central banks adjusting their lending rates up or down depending upon whether gold was flowing in or out. That system had kept prices and the exchange parities among major nations relatively stable. The

bankers who designed the system created by the Federal Reserve Act of 1913 hoped the gold standard would continue to
function this way.

As originally envisioned, the Fed's main purpose would be
to backstop the banks against runs on their deposits by supplying them with emergency loans. Disruptive events like the
series of bank runs in 1907 wouldn't be repeated and banks
would remain whole. Federal Reserve notes would provide
a national currency, giving the public greater certainty about
the validity of notes. The money supply would be governed by
the adjustments needed to keep the dollar price of gold steady,
which in turn would give the dollar a constant value.

But as the gold standard began to break down, with large
amounts of gold crossing the Atlantic Ocean to and fro, U.S.
monetary policy makers began to distrust the automatic
adjustment process. Monetary policy became more discretionary. That's where the trouble started with monetary management, as mere mortals tried to cope with the enormous
complexities of international monetary flows occasioned by
changes in the supply and demand for money.

This discretionary role was perhaps inevitable, given the
design of the Federal Reserve Act. Although the system of
twelve regional reserve banks was designed by bankers and
was intended to be independent of government, that's not
how things turned out. Congress and President Woodrow
Wilson ultimately took charge of the Federal Reserve bill and
shaped its final form so that it specified that seven "governors"
appointed by the president would sit in Washington and ensure effective political control. Leading bankers remonstrated

with the president in a stormy White House session over the potential for politicization of monetary policy, but he responded that letting bankers themselves control monetary policy would be like letting the railroads control their regulator, the Interstate Commerce Commission. He would have none of it.

The Fed, still a teenager in 1928, was not very good at the highly complex game of supplying the economy with the money it needed, not too much or too little. One could say that it is not very good at that job even today, well past its one hundredth birthday. From the beginning, the Fed was trying to regulate the nation's money supply in tune with the fluctuations of credit markets that are subject to powerful and unpredictable forces both domestic and foreign.

For example, American banks had large investments in Germany when it suffered hyperinflation in the 1920s, wiping out values denominated in marks. There were bright fellows at the Fed, but if they had been bright enough to manage such complexities we probably would not have had the deflation of the early 1930s and the recession of those years would have been mild enough that it would be a mere footnote in economic history, rather than the major event now known as the "Great Depression."

There is an argument that a power struggle between the able president of the New York Federal Reserve Bank, Benjamin Strong, and the system governors in Washington contributed to the confusion, although Strong died before the stock market crash. That argument is plausible in light of the fact that a struggle continues to this day between some of the more

independent-minded regional bank presidents, who are elected
by member banks, and the governors appointed by the president. Clearly, the presidential appointees are winning, as Woodrow Wilson meant for them to do. Did such a conflict play a role
in making the Fed impotent in 1930? Who knows? These were
mere humans, not gods.

All these events have led some analysts to believe the
country would have been better off if a central bank hadn't
existed in the 1920s and 1930s and even thereafter. They argue
that the United States grew smartly under the pre-Fed gold
standard but suffered more money and credit dislocations
after the Fed's 1913 debut. That argument has some flaws, for
example the question of whether a money system made up
of hundreds of different types of banknotes would have been
sustainable in a modern economy. But there is support for
it from the pickle the Fed has been in most recently. Having
forced interest rates down to near zero, thus grossly distorting
the credit markets and financing a doubling of the national
debt in just seven years, the Fed has feared making a move toward normality because it might cause another market crash.

CHAPTER SEVEN

★

BASHING THE BANKS

IN THE 1932 national elections, Hoover and his fellow Republicans in Congress had been trounced. Franklin Delano
Roosevelt became the new president and his Democratic Party
won control of Congress. FDR, in his March 4, 1933, inaugural
address, had sought to inspire Americans and lift them out of
their funk through the power of his silver tongue.

I don't know if anyone in my family heard FDR's address
on the battery-powered radio we used to listen to news, dance
music, and homespun comedy shows like *Lum and Abner*.
Our radio used a battery because we were still on the farm

west of Whiteland, four months before we moved to town and got electricity.

Historians favorably disposed toward the New Deal, of whom there are many, are fond of citing FDR's famous line, "[L]et me assert my firm belief that the only thing we have to fear is fear itself." They argue that these brave words inspired and raised the hopes of a demoralized nation. For all I know, they did for some. Certainly Roosevelt was a great orator and the new national radio station networks allowed him to reach any American who owned a radio, a technology-provided political gift not available to his predecessors and one he used quite effectively.

But there were some other parts of that speech that the New Dealers prefer to forget, because they were unsettling and probably did more to destroy confidence than build it. The new national leader stridently charged that "the rulers of the exchange of mankind's goods have failed through their stubbornness and their own incompetence, have admitted their failure and abdicated. Practices of the unscrupulous money changers stand indicted in the court of public opinion, rejected by the hearts and minds of men."

Bankers and business corporation executives who had knocked themselves out, literally, trying to cooperate with the government during the 1930 onset of the depression were now charged by the new president with blame for the sad state of affairs. Beautiful. He was invoking the parable of Jesus and the money changers in the temple to damn the U.S. banking and securities industry at a time when banks were dropping like flies as a result primarily of the erratic management of monetary policy by the government's central bank.

If his speech restored the confidence of the American people it sure didn't do much for the men who were trying to keep their banks afloat. The president's words were likely to have fanned the worries of depositors about the safety of the money they had placed in the hands of these vicious "money changers" and increased the chances for bank runs.

Not wanting to let a good crisis go to waste, the New Dealers launched "one hundred days" of legislative acts even more radical than those that had failed FDR's predecessor, Herbert Hoover. Confidence wasn't helped, either, by FDR's allusions in the speech to some vague scheme for taking people out of the cities and "engaging on a national scale in a redistribution endeavor to provide better use of the land for those best fitted for the land." That crazy idea was probably cooked up the wild-eyed Rexford Tugwell.

Nor were defenders of a constitution that had carefully defined and limited the prerogatives of American presidents likely to be inspired by his closing peroration that if all else fails, "I shall ask the Congress for the one remaining instrument to meet the crisis—broad executive power to wage a war against the emergency, as great as the power that would be given to me if we were in fact invaded by a foreign foe." In short, an American president was threatening to ask a rubber-stamp Congress dominated by members of his own party to grant him dictatorial powers.

If James and Sara Ollie Melloan had not bothered to listen to FDR's speech, it wouldn't be surprising. They were Republicans, a loyalty perhaps derived from their fathers, who both had chosen to fight in the Civil War on the side of a Republican president, Abraham Lincoln. The Civil War was a time when many of their fellow Kentuckians had thrown in their lot with the secessionist South, a split that led to heavy fighting in the state and the appellation "bloody Kentucky."

James and Sara had fared well, for a while at least, under Republicans in the 1920s. So in March 1933 they were still smarting from the defeat their party had suffered in 1932. They weren't fond of the new president with his patrician, upper-class eastern style of oratory.

Besides, they had better things to do. They were still in the farming business and it was springtime with a lot of work ahead. For Dad and the older boys, there was corn and wheat to be planted, using our team of horses, Billy and Fred, to pull the plows, farm disks, rollers, and planters. There were cows to be milked morning and night. For Mom, there was a kitchen garden to be planted, chickens to be fed, and a large family to cook for on our coal-fired kitchen range.

We farmed the old Davis place into the Depression but finally gave up and moved into town in late 1933. But before that, there was one last harvest, a time of joy and celebration for farmers down through the ages, at least when crops have escaped the hazards of washouts, drought, or disease. It was such for us in 1933, despite depressed prices for wheat, which was bringing only a pitiful 49 cents a bushel at the Whiteland elevator, compared with three times that amount in 1925.

As was the practice among midwestern grain farmers of that time, my father joined a threshing ring, made up of neighboring farmers with crops of wheat, rye, or oats. The group organized itself in late winter and contracted with the owner of a threshing machine to visit their farms at harvest time. They set up a schedule for the thresher to make the rounds of their farms, where they would cooperatively bring in the sheaves from the fields for threshing.

The threshing machine had been invented 150 years earlier by Scotsman Andrew Meikle, one of many machinery designers who participated in the industrial revolution. A revolving drum pressed the grain from the stalks and a vibrating conveyor separated it from the chaff and sifted it into a chute through which it was funneled into a truck or wagon alongside. A blower forced the remaining straw and chaff out a long metal tube, about a foot in diameter, that the operator could maneuver to create a straw stack. This machine became obsolete a few years after our harvest when farm equipment manufacturers, always competing to design more efficient machinery, invented self-propelled combines that moved through the fields harvesting and threshing the grain at the same time.

When my dad's wheat was threshed and loaded into the grain bed of a truck, it was hauled into Whiteland to the Valentine brothers' grain elevator. There Willie Graham, a friendly little man who was also the Presbyterian church organist, would have the driver pull onto the platform scales for weighing, after which his vehicle would be lifted at its front to slide the grain into an underground hopper, from whence it would be conveyed up and into the elevator by a chain of buckets. Then Willie would weigh the empty vehicle and subtract its empty weight from the previous loaded weight to get the weight of the grain. The amount was then credited to Dad's account at the current market value of the grain. The cash would help sustain our family until another harvest, except in this case another harvest never came. And the cash return, at the depressed grain prices of 1933, wasn't much. Dad made less than a hundred dollars after splitting with the farm owner and paying his share of the threshing costs.

Myron Brunnemer

But nonetheless, the arrival of the threshing crew in early July was the beginning of a glorious harvest day. First came the clanking threshing machine with the trademark J.I. CASE printed in big letters on its side, towed by a large steam tractor with cleated iron wheels. The tractor looked and puffed like a small train engine and even had a locomotive-style whistle that Myron Brunnemer, the owner and operator, would toot to announce his arrival. He would turn into our barnyard and position the thresher near where the straw stack was to be. Then a heavy drive belt was fastened in a figure-eight fashion between the drive wheel on the steam engine and the one on the threshing machine that actuated the contraption.

The farmers of the ring would then arrive, driving their teams and wagons, some of them standing up like chariot drivers and whipping their horses to a trot as they entered the lane to show off in front of their peers and the accompanying wives. The quality of their wagons and teams was a rough measure of how successful they were. One team of big black horses, with a silver caparisoned black leather harness, pulled a wagon that unlike the others still retained its green paint. That finery suggested that the owner, the lean, red-haired, and jolly Les Lyons, was either a very good farmer or heavily in debt, or perhaps both. His business survived the Depression, so the former was probably true.

The farm wives, arriving in the wagons with their spouses and baskets of food, would soon be busy setting up long plank tables, borrowed from a church hall, for the noon lunch. My sister Marie, two years my elder, and I contributed by lugging gallon jugs of water out to the wheat field to slake the thirst of the sweating men who were pitching the sheaves onto the wagons for hauling back to the threshing machine. Their horses were under remote control with the reins tied to the hayrack but they obeyed the commands of the working farmers of "hup" when it was time to move to the next stack or "wheat shock" of sheaves, and "whoa" when they reached it. The owner of the wagon would usually stay aboard to stack the sheaves, an important skill, since nothing could be more embarrassing than dumping a load of sheaves on the way to the thresher in the presence of the entire community. Bob remembers that someone found a black snake under a wheat shock and tossed it up to a loader. The joke was funny to everyone but the loader, who pitched it back.

At lunchtime, the steam engine would be powered down to a mere hiss and throb and the drive wheel disengaged; the men would unhitch and water their horses at the horse trough, giving them a helping of oats in their feedbags, and we would all have a jolly feast of fried chicken, ham, potato salad, bean salad, pies, and cakes, washed down with iced tea or lemonade made from real lemons. Then the men would lounge in the shade for a rest, swapping stories or local news as neighbors do, before returning to the field and the threshing. By late afternoon it was all over and the men and their wives in their empty wagons and food baskets headed home for dinner and a night's sleep, prepared to do the same thing at another farm the next day. Marie and I would admire the grand new twelve-foot-high straw stack that had materialized so quickly in our barnyard, suitable to play upon once it had settled and there was no danger of our poking holes that could cause the straw to collect water and rot.

★

CHAPTER EIGHT

FAREWELL TO SHARECROPPING

Meb and Bill

IN THE FALL, when the crops were all harvested, it was time for us to leave the farm. Farming, and particularly sharecropping, made no sense at the prices we had received for our products. Sharecropping, never an easy way to make a living, had become even less attractive under the New Deal's Agricultural Adjustment Act, passed in 1933. It took a lot of land that had been share-cropped out of production as part of its effort to raise prices by restricting supply. It prescribed federal cash subsidies for farmers who restricted their planting of corn, wheat, and other crops to the quotas authorized by Washington, but the subsidies didn't go to the people who farmed the land. They went to the owners.

This created anger among sharecroppers, particularly poor blacks in the South. But blacks had almost no influence in the politics of the South at that time, for the simple reason that they, often by means of deviously designed laws, were being denied their voting rights.

The Democratic Party dominated the southern states, a carryover from the Civil War, and the Democratic Party was in power in Washington. Southern legislators were heavily responsible for seeing to it that farm subsidies went to the owners. That of course affected sharecroppers everywhere, not just in the South. It curtailed what had been a traditional way for young couples to acquire land, first by sharecropping to learn the trade and then, after building a stake, finding land to buy. Farmers still sharecrop today but the common practice now is for large-scale farmers to share proceeds from land owned by nonfarmers, which is a form of rental and, if anything, places the owner, not the farmer, at a disadvantage. Modern equipment enables the renter to farm large acreages, numbered in the thousands compared to the hundreds or fewer in the 1930s. The owner wanting an income from his land often has no alternative but the farmer with the equipment and skill to farm it.

Our main reason for moving to town, however, was that my siblings had ideas other than farming for mapping out their careers. Melba was twenty-seven and well established at Kelly Chevrolet in Greenwood. Sis had graduated from Whiteland High School in 1930 and gone to Central Normal College in Danville for two years to earn her teaching certificate, the first member of our family to go to college. She was now teaching second grade at Whiteland, with the expense of paying Connie twenty dollars a month to ferry her back and forth from farm to school each day. Connie had a job maintaining and repairing slot machines, which were legal in Indiana at that time. Bill was itching to explore a wider world beyond Johnson County. Bob and Jim were in high school and Marie and I in grade school in Whiteland.

My older siblings, Bill in particular, were like young people of any era. They thirsted for adventure. It was a romantic age, the Depression notwithstanding. Hollywood movies had opened up new vistas. Style was important even in farm towns. Young people were poor, but goods were cheap, and under the influence of Hollywood they endeavored to dress well and drive the best cars they could afford. Harold K. "Sam" Battin, a Whiteland boy whom Sis would marry in May 1934, wore coveralls at the canning factory, but pinched pennies to buy his "good" clothes at L. Strauss & Co., the best men's store in Indianapolis. Sis and Sam made a handsome couple when they went out on a date, say, to the Circle Theater in Indianapolis. There they sat with a similarly well-dressed, and mostly similarly impecunious, audience to see and hear the big bands, or that great touring Broadway comedy extravaganza of the 1930s, Ole Olsen and Chic Johnson's *Hellzapoppin'*. Their favorite bandleader was Ted Lewis, the man with a battered top hat who asked, good times or bad, "Is everybody happy?" Sam's father, who really was named Sam, allowed them to use his late-model Dodge for their dates. Such a date could be managed for less than a dollar.

One of Sam's teammates on the 1929–30 Whiteland Wrens

basketball team, Woodrow "Woody" Sefton, had his own secret for dressing well. Woody had the slender athletic build
and fine facial features of a David Niven, and looked debonair
and confident enough to enter any place without being asked
what he was doing there. According to Sam, he improved
his wardrobe one day by walking into the Columbia Club, a
venerable and exclusive Indianapolis establishment on Monument Circle, and walking out wearing a far better overcoat,
camel's hair no less, than the one he came in with.

In short, Woody was a thief, although he grew out of those
bad habits. In the early thirties, when even the president of
the United States regularly excoriated the business wealthy,
stealing from the rich might be as likely to win admiration as
censure. That seemed to be the case with Woody.

Sam, brother Bill, and Sis graduated from Whiteland High
School in 1930. In their class picture, Sis stands behind Sam,
with her hand, barely visible, resting on his shoulder, a subtle
gesture of proprietorship. Bill and Sam were older than Sis but
Bill had lost some school time in the family's 1918 move from
Louisville. Sam, according to his daughter Sally, dropped out
of school a couple of times because he refused to submit to
the county public health nurse's inspections for head lice, a
common affliction for country kids of that era. Sam, a town
boy, considered such treatment beneath his dignity.

The motto of the Class of 1930 was "Grit Wins." Sis would
write later in Hugh Ross's book, "We were children of the Great
Depression, but our class motto was 'Grit Wins.' True grit was
a much-needed ingredient in our lives during those times. Jobs
were almost non-existent, and if you were lucky enough to find

a job, the prevailing wages were fifteen to twenty-five cents an hour. Our faces and our thoughts [referring to her class picture in the book] were sober because those were sober times. However, we lived up to our motto and Grit Won!"

My oldest siblings came of age in the 1920s, when the country was prospering under Harding and Coolidge and the automobile and movies were bringing about a cultural upheaval. Meb was a flapper, dressing herself in flimsy, short dresses, knee stockings, and cloche hats. She sometimes wore a bright orange satin pajama suit, modeled after the one Jean Harlow wore in the movies.

Connie at one point defied convention, and federal law, by engaging in a little bootlegging on behalf of Uncle Bert and his friends, who had a fondness for strong spirits that were then denied them by the Eighteenth Amendment to the U.S. Constitution. Connie procured the hooch by driving to a moonshine distillery, or "still," hidden in the hills of Brown County, a heavily wooded, lightly populated place south of our Johnson County. The project ended when Dad discovered his son's cache under the straw stack in our barn lot and was furious at Connie and his instigator, Uncle Bert.

Bob from an early age had a lifelong love affair with automobiles. He wrote me once to describe the various exotic types of cars that motored around Whiteland and Greenwood in the 1920s. I recalled a sleek white Cord with its long engine hood and wraparound chrome radiator grille owned by Tom Tribble, the Linco filling station proprietor. I also recall a little British Austin, whose owner I've forgotten.

Bob remembers what we called the old Chalmers. "It had

two jump seats that folded down from the back of the front seat. They were the place to sit if you were a kid. I couldn't believe it when Mom and Dad traded that car for a Model T Ford but the old Chalmers was prone to rear-end troubles whereas the T only required a set of transmission bands occasionally. A lot of our neighbors had Ts as well as big cars purchased in better times. John P. Trout had a Cole Eight, Russell Rund had a Gardner roadster, and my music teacher, Brownie Grubbs, drove a Marmon V-8. Sometimes she would take me home in that car, which was a thrill.

"We eventually traded the T for a 1926 Chevrolet touring car. It had enclosures made of plate glass and rigid frames, which was a big improvement over the old flapping side curtains. Melba drove this car a lot and she taught me how to drive."

Motorcycles fascinated the more adventuresome youths. An interest in airplanes was awakened when the Mullendore family turned part of their farm south of Franklin into a flying field, offering lessons in Piper Cub and Taylorcraft airplanes. With fast-moving machines available to thrill-seeking youths, there were of course fatalities. Local farm boy "Fats" Vehorn was killed on Highway 36 west of Indianapolis when his bike went out of control at 90 miles per hour. As a lark, he was trying to outrace the cops. Bob Foster crashed a Mullendore Taylorcraft showing off his flying skills over the family farm northeast of Franklin. He made the common error of a fledgling of banking sharply too close to the ground with insufficient flying speed. My friends and I rode our bicycles to the crash site. Someone asked a young man near the wreckage, "Did you know him?" He replied, "He was my brother."

My friend Billy Henry learned to fly when he was sixteen and took me for rides in the various planes available at Mullendores. We once went up in an open-cockpit PT-19. Billy flew over Whiteland and I took pictures with a Kodak. They turned out surprisingly well. Billy was a good driver and I fully trusted his abilities when we went skylarking.

Medical practice was far less advanced than now in those times. Connie, whose first car was a Ford roadster, tells this story of an experience in the late 1920s: "I was going up Road 31 one day and there was a wreck right north of Whiteland. The state patrol stopped me and asked if I would take a man to the doctor. He was redheaded and covered with blood. He had a cut on the back of his head about two inches long. He was a newspaper reporter out of Indianapolis. I took him to Dr. Woodcock in Greenwood.

"He [the reporter] was the worst guy to cuss that I ever saw. He got up on the table and Doc asked him if he wanted a painkiller. 'Hell no, go ahead and sew the damn thing up and get me out of here,' he said. Doc was nervous as a whore in church and every time he made a stitch the guy would cuss some more. Doc asked him about numbing it and he would cuss some more. When he got him sewed up and cleaned up, the guy gave me two dollars and sent me to Peeks Dry Goods to get him a shirt. He put it on and I took him across the street to the bus station. He boarded the bus still cussing and left town.

"I don't know what Doc charged him but it wasn't much. You could walk into most doctors' offices anytime and they were glad to visit with you. They didn't have many patients. Most of the sick people went to the drugstores. The druggists treated more people than the doctors. Harry Porter removed my tonsils by painting them with silver nitrate."

Connie may have been wrong about the silver nitrate *removing* the tonsils but it was an anti-infectant that might well have been used for treating tonsillitis. However, who knows? A caustic that powerful might well have destroyed the tonsil tissue although at some considerable risk of collateral damage.

Hugh Ross also tells of Harry Porter's doctoring services. When Hugh was in first grade he developed an infection at the base of his thumb. Instead of taking him to a doctor, his father took him to Harry. "Harry had me sit on a stool and rest my hand on the counter. Then with a quick motion of his knife he made a neat cut across the infected area of my thumb. All that yellow stuff oozed out and Harry wiped the wound clean with a cotton ball soaked with alcohol. He lifted a small gob of some antiseptic smelling salve from an open jar and put it on the wound."

Harry applied a bandage and Hugh was as good as new. Harry charged Connor Ross, Hugh's father, nothing for the service, explaining that he was not a doctor but maintained a first aid service for family and friends. The wound healed fine. Such was the state of the medical arts in the old days.

CHAPTER NINE

★

BILL HITS THE ROAD

IN 1930, THE United States was still in many ways an undeveloped nation. Since the population was only 123 million there were vast empty spaces, particularly west of the Mississippi. Except for those living in crowded city neighborhoods like New York's Hell's Kitchen, we Americans enjoyed a lot of elbow room and relished the idea of exploring our huge land. Modern automobiles and paved roads were great emancipators, giving a Hoosier the ability to visit exotic places like Miami, New Orleans, New York, or Washington, D.C., in the privacy of his car, for less than the fifty dollars it took to cover gasoline, food, and tourist cabins or even hotels in cities for a week's travel.

Los Angeles and San Francisco were a bit of a stretch because the roads through the western mountains and deserts were still often unpaved and treacherous, especially in winter. Even in good weather, driving to the West Coast from Indianapolis could require ten days of travel, with average speeds held down not only by bumpy roads but by the need to pass through towns and cities with low speed limits. Speed traps by the local cops in little towns in need of revenues were common. Urban bypasses were nonexistent. On the other hand, the American West from Kansas City onward to Los Angeles was lightly inhabited, so there were few small towns to slow you down. There were only about 25 million people, 20 percent of the total population, living in the entire vast American West at that time.

Travel adventures were possible mostly for those with sufficient cash and leisure, neither of which was freely available in the 1930s. Mobility was light-years ahead of what it had been in the horse-and-buggy days of thirty years before, but a lot less than the ranges of distances quickly traveled today in an era of freeways where you can motor at 75 miles per hour or fly in passenger jets that cover 500 miles in an hour.

But Depression or not, young people had an urge to explore, and if a job offered that prospect, what more could be asked? In the spring of 1933, while we were still on the farm, Bill heard from his high school buddy Ed Admire about a traveling job that offered high adventure. An Indianapolis auto dealer was looking for young men to chauffeur late-model used cars to Los Angeles, where automobile demand and prices were higher than in Indianapolis. It was a form of what economists would call arbitrage, making money on price disparities.

Los Angeles had enjoyed extraordinary growth in the 1920s on the back of an oil boom, the burgeoning movie industry, better means of shipping citrus products back east, and an influx of settlers and tourists attracted by the promotions of city boosters and the Southern Pacific Railroad. Its population had soared to 1,238,000 in 1930 from 576,000 a decade earlier, and it was already becoming what would distinguish it from the cities of the East and Midwest: a sprawling metropolis with limited public transport and thus a serious need for motorcars.

The Indianapolis drivers were being offered only fifty dollars, enough for bus fare and food to get themselves home with a little to spare, plus their expenses for gasoline, food, and lodging on the way westward. It was a challenging journey, much of it on unpaved roads through mountains and deserts. But jobs were hard to find in 1933 and so were glamour and excitement, particularly for farm boys. So Bill and Ed jumped at it. They would worry about getting back home when the time came.

They'd be drivers of a cavalcade of Chevys, Fords, and Dodges that would wend its way westward over narrow two-lane roads, passing through cities and towns but finding populated areas more scarce as they pushed on. There was not yet much of a federal road system as we know it, so their leader needed careful map study to avoid time-consuming detours into uncharted territory, traveling for miles on roads that led nowhere.

On June 22, 1933, Bill sent a penny postcard from Raton, New Mexico, to Mom, addressing it to Mrs. James *Malone*, Whiteland, Indiana. (Bill had decided to change our family name from the more unusual Melloan, and thus avoid the need to spell it for strangers. He would continue to do that throughout his life, but none of the rest of the family followed his lead.)

The card depicted an aerial view of the Raton Pass between Colorado and New Mexico, which at a 7,888-foot altitude was the gateway to the Southwest on what at that time was still called the Santa Fe Trail. Bill thought the scenery a "wonderful sight" and reported that "six of the cars got into the ditch this morning but I've been lucky so far, haven't had any trouble." Considering that he was traveling on treacherous mountain roads, this report was not entirely reassuring to his worried family, but to him it was a testimony to his driving prowess and sense of adventure.

Down off the mountain pass into Albuquerque, the caravan would join the famous Route 66 for the rest of their journey. As the old song goes, they got their kicks on Route 66. They would pass a restaurant called the Iceberg, which in fact looked like an iceberg stuck out in the middle of the desert. Native Americans were much in evidence with roadside offerings of turquoise bracelets, Indian blankets, and bolo neckties. Real cowboys herded cattle on the open range.

After its designation as a national highway in 1926, Route 66 had been heavily publicized as the best way "from Chicago to LA," by the "U.S. Highway 66 Association," a private group formed by businesses along the route. The association had placed an ad in the July 16, 1932, *Saturday Evening Post* inviting Americans in the more populated East and Midwest to drive their motorcars to the 1932 Los Angeles Olympics by way of Route 66. Quite a few did.

Contrary to popular belief, there were very few Joad families migrating to California in rattletrap trucks in the early 1930s, although there would be more after the 1934 and 1936 droughts in the Midwest, Arkansas, and Oklahoma. Most of the drivers were middle-class urbanites off on an adventure in what was to a degree the still-wild West. Some as well were in search of new opportunities for permanent residence in the Golden State.

Route 66 was far from being an interstate. Some parts were unpaved and there were long stretches of nothing in view but desert, punctuated by the occasional roadside restaurant or filling station. The drivers had to refuel frequently to avoid running out of gas in a remote area. Driving up mountains would often overtax the cooling systems of cars of that era, necessitating stops to let the steaming radiator cool off. Drivers often carried five-gallon cans of water to replenish coolant when driving through mountains and deserts. The steering on 1933 cars was often sloppy, creating yet another hazard when navigating sharp mountain turns. Cars of that era were a bit top-heavy, so rollover accidents were a danger.

An unpaved section of Route 66 through the Black Mountains outside Oatman, Arizona, presented a steep climb with a series of hairpin turns that were harrowing even for experienced drivers. Eastern tenderfoots sometimes hired local men to drive them over that stretch. Bill and Ed and their fellow drivers managed to negotiate it, though.

When the group got to Los Angeles and delivered their cars to local dealers, presumably turning a profit for the Indianapolis entrepreneur, the boys were on their own. Bill and Ed decided to use their cash to explore the West and make their way home by hitchhiking rather than by bus.

Bill sent his mother another of his rare postcards from Reno, Nevada, on July 9, showing Lake Tahoe as it looked then in all its wild and pristine beauty before being overwhelmed by hotels and casinos. Reno was already famous as the place where New York socialites and Hollywood movie stars went to get hitched or unhitched, thanks to Nevada's liberal marriage and divorce laws. The boys roamed the city, visiting its glittering gambling halls and hotels. Wrote Bill, "Say, this sure is a town, but I think we will drift toward home today. Don't know how long will take. Sis, Tell Evelyn [Sis's college roommate Evelyn McCullough] I still love her."

"Drifting" toward home was a lot harder than Bill imagined in what were still among the low months of the Depression, notwithstanding some small gains from the 1932 depths. He and Ed decided to split up, reasoning that drivers would be less wary of picking up a single young male than two. But the traffic to California in those days was heavily one-way, westward, as the great migration from distressed areas proceeded. Eastbound traffic was heaviest on Route 66. Having gone north to Reno, Bill had picked less traveled highways through even more remote areas. While hitchhiking, he learned that deserts could be hot in daytime and very cold at night, even in July. In some towns the police picked him up as a vagrant, but instead of putting him in jail for the night—which he might have welcomed—they just drove him to the other side of town and sent him on his way.

By the time he reached Omaha, Nebraska, he was broke and starving. He swallowed his jaunty pride and sent a collect telegram to the folks asking them to wire him money for bus fare and food. When Connie met Bill at the Greyhound bus station in Indianapolis, he was pale and gaunt. He would later demonstrate his thinness by showing his siblings that he could almost make his thumbs and forefingers meet circling his waist. But what an adventure! He had been to the fabled West of real cowboys, Indians, and Hollywood stars. It had been worth the rough trip home, although he never chose to talk much about that end of the voyage. Mom, to say the least, was very relieved to see him.

CHAPTER TEN

★

ELECTRIC LIGHTS

Aᴄ FTER BILL WAS safely home and the crops harvested, Dad
sold his team and farm equipment, and we loaded up a truck
with our belongings and moved into Whiteland. It was time for
us to get out of farming. Melba had found a big house adjacent
to the Presbyterian church that would accommodate us all

nicely. Meb, who was well established in the Greenwood business community by that time and was on good terms with the president of the Greenwood bank, came up with most of the money and arranged the mortgage on our in-town dwelling.

We brought some of the farm with us, including a Jersey cow, which Dad and the older boys continued to milk, and chickens, which Mom brought along for eggs and chicken dinners. In those days you didn't buy a frozen chicken from Frank Perdue. You first caught the chicken, using a long wire hooked at the end to snare its leg. Then you had to kill it. Mom was expert at wringing a chicken's neck and then chopping off its head with a hatchet. Usually the headless chicken would flop around for a while spasmodically, flinging blood in all directions, as its nervous system continued to function briefly. Then you had to scald it to loosen the feathers and pluck it. And finally you'd eviscerate it, extracting the gizzard, liver, and heart, and discarding the entrails, which hogs found to be delicious. Then you dipped the pieces in an egg and flour batter, heated a larded pan on the coal-fired kitchen range—or the coal oil (the name often used then for kerosene) stove in the summer kitchen if the season required—and fried them. Sometimes two chickens were needed when we were all assembled.

Our three-acre lot had a strawberry patch and in spring we planted a large garden as well, including potatoes and sweet corn for roasting ears. There was a lot of work to do, even in town, but we were used to it. Once, Dad wanted me to help him flick potato bugs off the plants into cans containing coal oil, the standard way of saving the plants from infestation. I suppose because of my aversion to both coal oil and bugs, I resisted.

Mom should have given me a whack and told me to get busy,
but instead she took my side. Dad was furious. I've always re-
gretted having had a role in one more defeat for my dad.

We had never lived in a house with electric lights, having
made do on the farm with coal oil lamps, although one utilized
a white "mantle" instead of a wick to give off a brighter light.
On our arrival in Whiteland, Marie and I took great delight in
flipping the light switch inside the front door to see the magical
bulb hanging from the front room ceiling go on and off. Mom
finally told us to stop, but in a gentle manner because she too
was obviously savoring the enjoyment of electric lighting after a
half century of nights illuminated only by the flickering flame of
coal oil lamps. I was pretty sure I was going to like town living.

We were soon actively engaged in the life of Whiteland. In
those days, small towns had distinct identities, their own cul-
tures, history, and legends. There was no television, so images
of distant places only intruded on our consciousness when we
read newspapers and magazines or watched the vivid newsreels at the Artcraft Theater in Franklin.

On the farm, our lives had been even more circumscribed.
We measured our domain by two big trees beside the gravel
road that passed our house, an elm one hundred yards to the
north and a beech the same distance to the south. On most
days, the only people we saw other than family were the occasional passersby on the road, like our farm neighbor old Newt
Barnes, whose bare knees sticking out of his overalls could
be seen projecting above the door of his Model T, a sight that
amused us greatly.

In town it was quite different. Whiteland was a small town

but a far more varied and interesting domain than the farm. We had the school, the shops, and the workplaces. Marie and I delighted in getting to know our new habitat and its people. We were often assigned to pick up the mail at the post office, where Mildred Shinn was the postmistress. The post office was the nexus of our village because everyone had a box there and usually chatted with Mrs. Shinn about local happenings. She would see to it that the bad news of sickness or adversity was passed along, and also any good news of wedding engagements or the arrival in town of interesting newcomers.

The Whiteland Cafe next door was a place to spend a nickel on a Coke or dish of ice cream. Old John Earhart, an elderly, pudgy German, ran the grocery store on the corner. A double door slanted across the corner led into his domain. He specialized in slicing baloney and spiced ham so thin that it bunched up and gave the appearance of more meat than was actually there. Interestingly, it also seemed tastier that way.

Earhart had seen worse times, too, during the Great War, when Germans were suspected of being potential saboteurs and President Wilson ordered a young Bureau of Investigation prodigy named J. Edgar Hoover to detain suspect Germans. J. Edgar assiduously rounded up thousands, most of whom were innocent of even disloyalty, let alone crimes. It was a precursor to an even more extensive roundup twentyfour years later of Japanese-Americans after the attack on Pearl Harbor, in both cases a stain on American democratic practice, standards of due process, and protection of property.

Earhart, although not interned, had to bear the burden of the enmity the roundup and the war inspired. But in the

1930s, he was a cheerful presence and well accepted in our town, although townspeople sometimes gossiped that he weighed his thumb with the lunch meat. But then all grocers had to bear that suspicion.

Grocery clerks in today's big box stores are absolved of such doubts because they aren't the owners and hence cheating would afford them no profit. The anonymous owners don't escape blame for rising prices or other inconveniences but they, unlike the clerks, don't have to face the unhappy customers directly. Small-town grocers of yore were owners who lived side by side with their customers and had to bear directly the burden of any complaints. It exercised a certain discipline over their business methods.

The double screen doors of Earhart's store were decorated with orange enameled metal push-pull bars advertising Yum Yum bread. Outside on the sidewalk was a matching orange-painted box with a metal covered lid to receive the fresh bread that the Yum Yum truck from Indianapolis delivered in the early morning before the store opened.

The old Thompson Hotel, a long two-story frame building alongside the railroad tracks, had once provided lodging for commercial travelers when the railroads were the principal means of travel and passenger trains stopped in Whiteland and other small towns. It had long since been converted into small apartments, most of them occupied by young wedded couples. Sis and Sam set up housekeeping there when they first married. Nearby, Shelby Duncan, the town shoe cobbler, was a friend indeed when your feet were getting wet from water leaking through worn-out soles. What a pleasure it was to be reshod with new leather soles and rubber heels.

Across the tracks from Shelby, the small brick building owned by United Telephone Company had housed a telephone operator in the 1920s but in 1928 it had been automated. It just sat there, locked and unoccupied, quietly handling calls made and received on Whiteland's party lines. I sometimes marveled at the idea that something useful was going on in a locked building empty of people. That was my first encounter with electronic telecom technology, vintage 1933.

Across Main Street from the exchange was the grocery and dry goods store owned by Flora and Homer Fisher, who were aided by Flo's sturdy, cheerful nephew from Franklin, Charlie Littleton. Flo and Charlie, wearing white aprons, handled the grocery trade, slicing meat and extracting canned goods from the higher shelves using a pole with a gripper on the end that could be closed around a can by squeezing a handle at the bottom end of the pole.

Homer had the lighter duty of manning the separate room where work clothes, straw hats, gloves, yard goods, and sundry other items were offered. Outside, there was a Standard Red Crown gas pump and, next to the store, a tank of coal oil. I remember it well because one of my chores was to take the one-gallon glass coal oil container from our stove in the summer kitchen to have it filled, for which Mrs. Fisher charged fifteen cents. The coal oil invariably slopped over during the filling and coated the outside of the container. The oil on the container brushed off on my bare legs as I lugged it home. From age seven, I never liked coal oil.

Flo was all business on the job, but she had a light side as well, or maybe just an advanced appreciation of the value of good community relations, what today we call PR. Every Easter she would stage an Easter egg hunt in a vacant lot she owned, making sure that even the most clueless moppets managed to find a few eggs. Most children found their way to the hunt without parental aid, the little ones accompanied by older siblings or the older children of neighbors, there being little worry in a small town about letting children move about on their own. Flo seemed to enjoy the excitement as much as did the youthful seekers. When a child reached the age of twelve, Flo would "graduate" him or her from the Easter egg hunt with the present of a leather-bound New Testament.

Just northeast of Fishers' on an otherwise vacant lot stood the little shack that was home to Lee and Hattie Brown. The Browns, in their early sixties, were a bit of a mystery to townspeople because they had no visible means of support. Their shabby appearance offered hints of onetime gentility. Indeed, they might once have been a handsome couple. Lee, straight and thin, dressed himself in a brown three-piece suit, albeit one that was well worn. Hattie wore a hat, also the worse for wear and years out of style. They were always seen together and had no social standing, unless you would consider being at the rock bottom of society standing of a sort.

They seldom communicated with others and were sometimes harassed by mean little boys who threw rocks at their shack. We knew that they fed themselves in summer with late-night raids on local gardens. But otherwise we had little idea of how they got by. All we knew is that they did somehow get by, a testimony to human survivability, even during a depression. They also were a reminder that social mobility goes in two directions, both up and down.

A block east of the telephone exchange was the town's icehouse, owned by the Alexander Coal & Ice Company, based in Franklin. Most Whiteland families used iceboxes for refrigeration because they couldn't afford modern refrigerators. Raymond "Johnny" Park, who taught mathematics at Whiteland High School, supplemented his income by delivering ice in summer. Johnny was slender but strong and was well conditioned from carrying as much as one hundred pounds of ice in a canvas sling that he hefted onto his back.

Customers put a square card printed clockwise with four numbers, 25, 50, 75, and 100, in their front windows. The householder turned the card so that the number designating how much ice was wanted would be at the top. Johnny just looked at the number and brought in the ice. There was almost always someone home in an age when few housewives worked outside the home. If not, no one locked doors, so the iceman would just walk in and fill the icebox, collecting later. Johnny would give kids ice chips to suck on while he was chipping hundred-pound blocks to the desired size.

We never knew where the ice originated, but I suppose it came from northern lakes in insulated railcars in winter to the larger Alexander icehouse in Franklin. Or maybe there was an electric freezer somewhere that could produce hundred-pound chunks. I never heard of one.

The rail depot northward of the Fishers' on what was called the county road no longer handled passenger traffic but it did deal with freight. The Stokely canning factory farther up the county road was Whiteland's only real industry. It employed a few people year-round to do maintenance and warehouse work. But in that glorious season of summer, it become a very busy place, employing numbers of townspeople in a series of packing periods, especially during the tomato pack. It was the primary market for the fresh vegetables raised by area farmers.

Westward to Highway 31 and the Interurban "car line" was what we called New Whiteland, although some of it was pretty old. Whereas old Whiteland sprouted alongside the railroad tracks in the mid-nineteenth century, before automobiles, New Whiteland had emerged after motorcars began coming into use in the 1910s and '20s, creating traffic on Highway 31. One of the oldest buildings in New Whiteland was John Scott's general store at the corner of 31 and Whiteland Road. It was a concrete-block building with a wooden canopy in front sheltering a long bench for any loafers who weren't troubled by lazing six feet away from a busy highway. John Scott, the former Ferris wheel impresario, was known around town for the frugality he inherited from his Scottish ancestors.

When he retired from the carnival business, he had saved enough to buy this store and two nice houses in Old Whiteland, one to live in and one to rent out for a steady income. He, his wife, and daughter, Fern, manned the musty store from dawn to dusk, each day except Sunday walking back and forth the quarter mile between their home and store. They led a quiet life, mainly because they didn't have many customers. Walking into their store was a bit like interrupting a quiet family gathering. Yet they got by.

Fern was a cosseted young woman, pretty but pale and timid. Her hair, like her mother's, was braided into a long pigtail and her homemade dresses were about fifteen years out of style. Once she was walking alone from the car line and L. B. McAtee, the handsome and virile agriculture teacher at the high school, stopped his car and offered her a ride. Fern accepted but once inside the car she shrank against the passenger door and uttered the words much quoted by town boys thereafter: "Don't you touch me!"

The Scotts were memorable also for the time they took a tubful of coins to the bank in a wheelbarrow. The tub had been beneath the floor near the cash register for years and each time they made a sale they had dropped a nickel into the tub through a slot in the floor. Over time, it added up. I don't know how much was credited to their account when they deposited the tub of coins, but it was a lot more than most people today would take to the coin sorter at Stop & Shop.

On the southeast corner of Whiteland Road and Highway

31 was Tom Tribble's Linco filling station. Linco was one of the brands of Ohio Oil Company, later subsumed under the name Marathon. It was a handsome station, dressed up in a siding of white-enameled metal panels that gave it a glow.

Tom had a nice station but didn't do as much business as the Gulf station northward up the highway owned by Marley Williams and managed by "Babe" Baughman, who had been a Whiteland High basketball player in the late 1920s and had many friends and admirers. Marley knew what he was doing when he hired Babe.

Across the highway from Babe's was a little Red Rose station that only pumped gas and sold oil, candy, and cigarettes. Unlike its competitors it offered no repairs or oil changes. It was usually manned by "Alma," the voluptuous and not unattractive, but somewhat uncivilized, young wife of an elderly man named Wilson. They were recent arrivals from Kentucky.

Alma matter-of-factly used words seldom heard in either polite or impolite company. Even Sam Battin, whose shock threshold was high, was sometimes taken aback by her explicitness. Alma didn't seem to realize that she was making social errors. She simply used Anglo-Saxon words that have described parts of the human anatomy since Shakespeare. Or maybe I'm being too kind and Alma was totally aware that her choice of words was sometimes shocking. Maybe she found pleasure in that awareness. Connie found her charming.

Also on the highway was Gray's furniture and hardware store, operated by a large, personable, and courteous man named Paul Hand, a nephew of the founder. Paul, unlike most merchants, wore a suit, since selling furniture was a big-ticket business worthy of some formality. An overstuffed sofa in 1933 might cost as much as thirty dollars, so it was two weeks' wages for a lot of Whitelanders. The hardware section in the back of the store was usually manned by a hired hand attuned more to the needs of local carpenters than upmarket housewives. In between Gray's and Scott's stores was the Whiteland Inn, a restaurant. Across the highway from the Linco station was yet another grocery, which would figure into the Melloan family history, of which more later.

Another filling station, this one Standard Oil of Indiana, was on 31 south of the Whiteland Road. Our five general stores meant we had a variety of places to shop for groceries and dry goods, and our six gasoline stations, counting the pumps in front of Fisher's and McIntire's garage, gave us similar latitude in buying fuel. Such abundance made the vending of food and fuel sufficiently competitive to keep prices in check, but then the Federal Reserve System had done most of that work by allowing the deflation that had sent prices plunging from their 1929 level.

We also had three churches, Presbyterian, Methodist, and Baptist, one for every 133 souls, if you don't count the country folks who drove in for services and in fact usually outnumbered the townspeople who attended church. That should have kept us sufficiently pious, one would think, although that was not always evident. But don't underestimate the importance of churches in the development of the U.S. economic and social structure.

★

CHAPTER ELEVEN

BALM TO THE SPIRIT

THE EARLY SETTLERS in Johnson County, as in much of the country in the eighteenth and nineteenth centuries, spent their days doing hard physical labor under arduous conditions. Before they could plant crops, they had to clear the land of trees and brush and lay field tile to drain water from the many swampy areas into the creeks and rivers that crisscrossed the landscape. They built roads sometimes using the "corduroy" method of laying logs crosswise to float, in a sense, across swampy patches, an expedient that was not always successful.

The roads often followed old Indian trails. The "three-notch" road from Morgantown to Indianapolis, now State Highway 135, was so named for its early trail markings. Some early roads were marked with poles with painted rings. Pioneers lived rough in a life-draining malarial environment, beset by snakes and mosquitoes, hardly the pristine natural existence that environmentalist utopians dream of today. Lives were short, certainly by today's standards. Even in the 1930s, anyone in his sixties was regarded as elderly.

That perhaps explains why building churches was among the highest priorities of pioneers. They craved a gathering place where they could socialize and find comfort with their neighbors, talk about solutions to common problems, and give their children schooling. The daily grind of physical labor and the coarseness of life drew them to the refinements of worship. Sunday was a day of much-needed rest and a time to elevate themselves above the grit and grime of farm labor by dressing in their best clothes, the men in suits and ties and the women in sober dresses. They could listen to music from an organ and choir and sing hymns. The experience was meant to be uplifting and it usually was.

The Presbyterian church was next door to our house. In the 1930s, most of my family skipped church although Dad and Mom had once been active in the rural Honey Creek Church, west of Greenwood, which still exists. But Marie and I enjoyed meeting our friends at Sunday school and stayed for the service. Willie Graham, who on weekdays took charge of the grain and coal shipments in and out of the Whiteland elevator, on Sunday played the pipe organ while other members of the Graham family, including patriarch Charlie, added their musical talents to a sizable choir. It was indeed stirring to hear them lead the congregation in singing, "Let Mount Zion rejoice! Let the daughters of Judah be glad!" with Emma Boone, a pretty dark-haired spinster who worked somewhere in the city weekdays, soaring above the rest with her excellent soprano voice.

Emma was the star of the choir on Sunday mornings, but on weekdays, on her way home from the car line, she betrayed signs of stress and maybe depression. A solitary woman, she sometimes wobbled a bit on her high heels, a suggestion that she had had a highball or two before boarding the Interurban to come home. No one seemed to be close to Emma and she seemed not to welcome friendship. The Boones lived in a big painted brick house east of the church. Apparently they had once had money, and maybe still did. Three other pretty daughters married happily. Emma and her parents were more reclusive.

Roy Sharp, a Presbyterian elder who farmed a big spread for that time, 210 acres, and shepherded it through the Depression, had a sentimental side. He was sometimes so moved while serving Communion that he shed tears. Farmers were hardened by physical labor and the exigencies of the times, but that didn't mean they were bereft of soft human emotions.

Alas, that sturdy old brick church, with its stained glass windows and magnificent array of golden organ pipes behind the choir stalls, caught fire one night in 1946 and was gutted, leaving just an empty shell. Whiteland was lessened by the tragedy.

CHAPTER TWELVE

AIN'T WE GOT FUN

Modern accounts tend to treat the 1930s as a dismal decade, and for some Americans it was. But like other decades of our history, it was also a decade of rewarding accomplishments that contributed to the richness of our culture. The talented musicians at the Presbyterian church were not an exception. Whiteland, the educational and cultural focal point of Pleasant

Township, had a musical tradition. Professor Harold Hill of
Meredith Wilson's *The Music Man* was a fake but our music
teachers and bandleaders knew their business. And, paraphras-
ing the movie, "that band was in uniform, too."

A picture in Hugh Ross's book showing Merrill Henry's
seventy-member Johnson County 4-H band turned out in
braided tunics and white trousers is rather amazing in what
it says about the ability of those old bandmasters to mobilize
young talent, not to mention the willingness of people with not
much money to spend some of it on uniforms and instruments.

In summer, the 4-H band gave Saturday night concerts
at the Franklin courthouse square to entertain the masses
of country people who flocked to town to do their weekly
shopping, socialize, or attend a movie. Farmers would often
have spent the afternoon at the sale barn selling or buying
hogs, cattle, or farm implements. *Life,* a highly popular
Time Inc. picture magazine of the pre-TV era, featured the
doings of Whiteland farmer Glenn Dunn's family, four boys
and a girl, in a 1936 picture story about the Franklin Saturday night.

There were other sources of entertainment. Also on Saturday nights, there were square dances to country music at the
Whiteland Barn, an establishment on the county road north
of the canning factory operated by the Holt family, who also
grew dill for the pickle industry in a field below the barn.

The dances were patronized mostly by folks from Indianapolis who wanted to sample rural life. They were usually
shunned by the God-fearing farmers who actually lived rural
lives. That was because the barn had a reputation as a place

where revelers brought whiskey and mixed it with their Cokes and 7-Ups. They sometimes got rowdy.

The Holts dealt with this by hiring Bill Veatch, a Whiteland bachelor, as bouncer. Bill was a large, good-tempered man who was much admired around Whiteland for his carpentry skills. He built houses single-handedly, and it was said that in joining wood together, places where only one nail might do got two nails from Bill. His houses were sturdy and built for the ages. His imposing size, strong arms, and gentle nature were the perfect combination for pacifying obstreperous drunks.

High school basketball was the main winter attraction, a reflection of what came to be called Hoosier Hysteria, the state's basketball mania at high school tournament time. *Look* magazine in 1944 recorded this phenomenon with a picture article centered on the Whiteland team. Remarkably the Dunn family figured in both the *Life* and *Look* magazine stories, with my classmate Dick Dunn and his siblings in the *Life* article and Dick as a guard on the Whiteland Warrior team in the *Look* piece. Having one of Whiteland's families featured in two separate national magazines was a distinction that caused great pride in Whiteland.

And then there were family picnics and church penny suppers. Nearby Greenwood had its own amateur repertory theater company that performed at the Community House, a building donated by one of the town's earlier entrepreneurs, James T. Polk. Other would-be thespians gave dramatized "readings" at social functions. At the Whiteland gun club, shotgun owners demonstrated their prowess at popping clay pigeons. Auction bridge, euchre, and dances also were popular at the club.

In summer, a family-run "medicine show" would visit Whiteland, pitching a tent in a vacant lot on the east edge of town. Admission was free to what was rather good entertainment, music, dancing, and clowning. The show made its money by selling a "tonic" called Molax at a dollar a bottle, less as the night wore on and additional supplies were offered to buyers at a deep discount. My guess is that the "tonic" vended by medicine shows during Prohibition was popular because of its alcoholic content. Vendors deliberately set up in small towns like Whiteland, with no law enforcement officials who might ask questions. The shows continued to tour for a few years even after Prohibition was repealed in 1933 but then died out.

Hugh Ross, a talented trumpet player himself who performed in jazz bands and orchestras, describes the medicine show fondly in his book. He wrote that it was mostly a family affair with the father playing banjo and a one-man band contraption, the mother playing violin, banjo, and concertina, and their teenage daughter tap dancing. There were two other musicians, one on trombone and the other on clarinet, piccolo, fife, kazoo, and various whistles. All members of the company sang and danced.

Wrote Hugh: "Imagine their orchestration of banjo, washboard, trombones, clarinet, kazoo and vocal doing 'Back Home Again in Indiana' or 'Alexander's Ragtime Band' at a good Dixieland clip. My favorites of the outfit (along strict musical lines) were the two hired hand wind players with the names of Jake Whippersnapper and Enic Spinckt. Jake played a good 'tail gate' style and his stage role was 'top banana.' A favorite gag was that he had a second trombone with a horizontal curved slide; he could play correctly while marching around corners. Enic's stage role was as the stooge, but his timing in switching instruments for special effects was brilliant."

Not so entertaining, but nonetheless fascinating, was a medicine man who sometimes set up a stand next to the firehouse. He was, or at least was dressed as, a Native American in full headdress with a certain resemblance to a cigar store wooden Indian. His specialty was a medicine that cured and/or prevented gastrointestinal parasites. I would pass his stand on my way to school in the morning and would be both intrigued and repelled by the display on his little counter, jars filled with tapeworms supposedly removed from human innards. It set me to thinking about how horrible it would be to have such a creature in my alimentary canal. I assume he made a few sales to adults with similar concerns, probably also medicine with a generous amount of alcohol, but I never saw anyone actually buy his medicine.

While we enjoyed these small-town entertainments, we were also looking out on a broader American culture that was far from stagnant. Babe Ruth, that legend of the 1920s, was still hitting home runs for the Yankees in the 1930s, on his way to a record career total of 714. Jesse Owens, the great track star, would win fame at the 1936 Olympics, much to Hitler's chagrin. Joe Louis, the "Brown Bomber," would stun Hitler once more in June 1938 by knocking out German boxer Max Schmeling, who had defeated him in 1936, in a bout staged in Yankee Stadium that attracted worldwide interest. Louis dispatched the German in just over two minutes.

Technology continued to advance. Air travel became safe and practical thanks to the new two-engine, all-metal passenger planes, first the DC-2 and then the DC-3, developed by Douglas Aircraft. DuPont developed an artificial rubber fabric called Neoprene in 1931 that advanced a new industry, plastics, that had been born in the 1920s with the advent of Bakelite. The main two-hundred-mile stretch of the Pennsylvania Turnpike, from near Harrisburg to Pittsburgh, was built in a mere two years, from October 1938 to October 1940. By contrast, the New York World Trade Center, destroyed by Arab terrorists in September 2001, was not yet fully replaced fifteen years later, thanks to regulation and political maneuvering.

Despite the Depression and the New Deal, America was a dynamic place in the 1930s. A still-popular song in the 1930s was that 1921 show tune by Richard Whiting, Raymond B. Egan, and Gus Kahn: "Ain't We Got Fun?" Well, actually we did have fun, Depression or not.

★

CHAPTER THIRTEEN

LITTLE BIG MAN

Ralph Barger

Economic professors, or at least some of them, spend a lot of time studying the workings of markets and passing along what they have learned to students. In 1933, the United States was being led by a president who had even less faith in markets than his predecessor. His "brain trust" thought that superbright people, such as themselves, could do a better job of managing the allocation of scarce resources than the invisible hand of the market. They had set about to prove it in the big package of legislation that would soon make itself felt in our town and others throughout the nation.

In Whiteland, we were backward and still doing things the old-fashioned way but with a high degree of economic efficiency and amazingly good results. One of our best prac-titioners of free market economics, in its very simplest form, was a little man named Ralph Barger. Ralph was a hunch-backed dwarf whose face was often blackened by coal dust, because he made his living in fall and winter hauling coal in his one-horse wagon from the railroad coal yard to the coal bins of Whiteland homes. Today Ralph would be considered "handicapped" and deserving of pity. But in that long-ago time, he was a businessman like his full-size peers, only a bit more interesting.

He sometimes lunched at the Fishers' store on a ten-cent baloney sandwich and a five-cent half-pint bottle of milk, looking up at other customers speculatively from under his ancient, coal-stained black leather cap. Before he left he would buy a couple of two-for-a-nickel King Edward cigars, later smoking them down to the last two inches and chewing the rest to get his full two and a half cents' worth.

He was a solitary man, but one who had come to terms with his affliction. He had learned to manage his horse, which was so docile it always looked bored. To climb aboard his wagon, he would put one foot on a spoke of the front wheel and hoist himself up, using the spoke as a ladder. If the horse moved even slightly during this exercise, he would roar "Whoa!" and the horse would obey. There was no record of Ralph ever having pitched to the ground by an untimely move by his horse. He was remarkably agile for such a deformed man, and muscular, hardened by years of shoveling coal. He made other deliveries as well and seemed to be about as busy in warm weather as cold, carting away junk, for example, to a bin where it would be picked up by a junkman from Indianapolis.

Ralph lived alone in a small farmhouse on the Tracy road some two miles northeast of Whiteland. He had had a strange upbringing. His parents garbed him in dresses when he was young, presumably to try to hide his deformity. His father had died in a shotgun blast and there was a legend that Ralph had pulled the trigger, either accidentally or deliberately, and had thrown his dead father down a well. That story made him an awesome character even though he seems to have been exonerated and had led an exemplary life since the tragedy. Two country girls who lived up the road from Ralph, Dorothy Jean Thompson (later Melloan after she and Bob married) and Grace Speas, said they always sped up in fear when they rode their bicycles past his house.

Hugh Ross had no such concerns. He writes about riding with Ralph on one of his daily rounds when Hugh was an adventuresome and inquisitive youngster. To start a run, Ralph would maneuver his horse and wagon alongside the open coal car on a siding of the Pennsylvania Railroad track. He was about the height of his short-handled scoop shovel but that didn't limit his capacity to shovel coal. Wrote Hugh:

"Ralph would load his wagon and pull into the scale shed to receive the 'bill of lading' made out to Jack McIntire for 962 pounds of Pocahontas coal from Pennsylvania. This was the very best lump coal available. Due to the haul distance by Pennsylvania Railroad, it was also the most expensive—i.e., $7 a ton, or $3.50 per 1000wt which equals .0035 cents per pound. Ralph paid for Jack's coal (962 X .0035) in the amount of $3.37, tendering four one dollar bills from his long, vertical, black leather snap purse.

"When the invoice and 63 cents change were passed back through the window, he carefully put the invoice and the 50-cent piece in his purse. That purse was for 'big money' and important papers. The 13 cents was knotted in the corner of his handkerchief. Then the office manager, Willie Graham, told Ralph that he had an order from Zeb Adams for 100 pounds of chicken mash which he may as well take along on this trip. The two fifty-pound bags were 75 cents each; Ralph traded back the 50 cents piece plus another paper dollar for Zeb's chicken feed bill.

"With the office work business over, Ralph pulled into the elevator shed and the 'Millman,' John Yaste, put the two sacks for Zeb into the 'cab' alongside of Ralph. There was still room for more. Before Ralph could make another move the RR Depot manager walked in and told Ralph that he had a keg of nails for Gray Furniture and Hardware. Although a keg of nails took about the same space as a sack of flour it was very much heavier—too heavy for most of us to carry across two sets of railroad tracks. Ralph, therefore, would [circle by road to] the railroad freight dock.

"The RR manager would bring the nail keg across the boardwalk with a two-wheel dolly and load it by the side of Ralph and the two sacks of grain in what we can fairly call the 'cab' of Ralph's freight wagon. Webster's definition of 'cab' is: 'A place in a truck where the operator sits.' . . . Ralph, however didn't sit. He stood upright and rested his elbows on a wooden box-type dashboard, which supported his hands and controlling reins of his horse. In this way he was in a relaxed but ready attitude. (I cannot ever recall seeing Ralph sitting down.) Ralph was now loaded for a common-place trip to what we called 'West Whiteland!' . . .

"Jack McIntire's auto repair garage was behind his house. As Ralph unloaded the last of the coal shipment to Jack's coal bin, Jack came out from his shop and said: 'Hang on for a few minutes, Ralph, while I gather up some trash that needs hauling off.' Ralph charged Jack $3.37 for the coal, plus 35 cents for delivery plus 15 cents for hauling the trash. 'That's a four dollar bargain,' said Jack.

"At Zeb Adams['s] garden, across the street and down an alley from Jack's, Zeb presented Ralph with two apples, one for him and one for his horse. Zeb raised chickens as well as starting vegetable plants in early spring to sell to other gardeners and farmers. He bartered his surpluses of eggs and pullets, after feeding his own family, to local groceries in return for flour, milk and other necessities.

"Ralph tendered his bill on the elevator invoice as before. The bill was $1.50, plus 15 cents (delivery), which equaled $1.65. Zeb gave Ralph $1.75 in three coins, a silver dollar, fifty cent piece and quarter. Ralph pulled out his handkerchief to make change. Zeb wanted Ralph to keep the change but Ralph insisted. He would only take the money he was entitled, consistent with his charges to all customers. Zeb accepted the dime change but reached down behind a bush, picked up a small basket of sweet potatoes and placed it in the cab. Ralph was pleased with the gift and transferred the potatoes into a spare gunny sack and returned the basket to Zeb. This concluded a business deal between two wealthy men."

Thus went an episode in the commerce of a small town on a nice day in the 1930s. Ralph was a throwback to an earlier era, but he nonetheless provided a valuable service. One night years later, Wayne McIntire (Jack's son) and I were heading out of town eastward in Jack's 1940 Chevy to pick up two country girls who were our dates for the night. We came up behind Ralph in his wagon, with a lighted lantern swinging from the rear. Ralph turned and faced our headlights with an expression that looked like anger, or maybe fear, since his little wagon was no match for Jack's car in a collision. It occurred to me as we passed that we are going out with two pretty girls to see a movie and afterward we would park on a country lane to chat and "neck," the expression at that time, and maybe even now, for hugging and kissing. Ralph, by contrast, would go to his little house, unhitch, feed, and water his horse, have a solitary meal, probably just cold meat and bread, and then lower his deformed body into bed in goodness knows what position that would allow a comfortable sleep. Life is unfair.

But maybe Ralph didn't see it quite that way. He was a respected businessman who provided a valuable service to the community. He made his own way without anyone's help. Clearly he took pride in that and didn't want anyone's pity. Maybe he was happier in his own skin than one would have imagined.

CHAPTER FOURTEEN

★

WHITELAND'S TRUCKERS

Rᴀʟᴘʜ ʙᴀʀɢᴇʀ ᴡᴀꜱɴ'ᴛ the only businessman in Whiteland to make a living in transport. Some Whiteland men had been quick to seize upon a new opportunity, long-distance trucking.

Trucks had brought great benefits as a farm tool in the 1920s, enabling farmers to haul their products longer distances than were possible with horses and wagons, giving them more outlets to dairies, grain elevators, and canning factories and hence more bargaining power with processors. Truck builders like Ford, Dodge, Chevrolet, and International

Harvester (now Navistar) competed through the 1920s and
'30s to build better trucks, safer, more powerful, and able to
carry heavy loads long distances.

Even during the Depression, farmers who could raise $900
found a new truck a good investment because, thanks to the
competition among truck builders to design more advanced
models each year, it would do more work than an old truck.
They also had learned that a modern truck could be a profit
center in ways other than seasonal farm-to-market hauling.

Whiteland became something of a trucker's town after
Prohibition was repealed in 1933. Sturdy Ford and International "straight" trucks with grain beds became an efficient
way to haul grain from the elevators of Indiana and Illinois
to the newly reactivated bourbon distilleries of Kentucky. The
distilleries didn't buy closer to home because Kentucky's poor
soil was not optimal for growing grain. After unloading the
grain at the distilleries and collecting their fees, the truckers
could drive over to the mines of eastern Kentucky and pick up
a load of coal to haul back home to the trackside coal yards,
which often were adjacent to the elevators and owned by the
same firms. Most people at that time relied on coal for both
heating and fueling the kitchen ranges where they cooked
their food.

The truckers proudly displayed their names and the words
"Coal and Grain" on the doors of their trucks. It was rumored
that one Whiteland trucker had wives and families in both
Kentucky and Whiteland, much as in the charming 1953
movie *The Captain's Paradise,* about a ferryboat captain (Alec
Guinness) who has a homebody wife in Gibraltar (Celia John-

son) and a lover (the saucy Yvonne De Carlo) in "Kalique," Morocco. If the Whiteland story was true and the trucker's coal and grain trade was supporting two families, it must have been profitable.

Tom Kelsay, a farmer-trucker in the coal and grain trade who was a good friend of Sis and Sam, sometimes brought Sam a bottle of whiskey from a small, obscure distillery he supplied in Loretto, Kentucky. Sam let me taste it, even though I was several years underage, and it was remarkably smooth. It later became a premium brand, Maker's Mark, now marketed by a Japanese company, Suntory.

My brothers Jim and Bob both found jobs out of high school driving for Whiteland truck owners. When I was eleven, Jim once invited me to go along when he drove Tom Kelsay's truck to an elevator in Chrisman, Illinois, to pick up a load of wheat. Driving out State Route 36, a straight shot from Indianapolis to Chrisman, Jim asked me to hold the wheel while he lit his pipe. I complied with this startling request, but not proficiently. While he calmly fired his pipe tobacco, Jim said, "Don't look at me, look at the road." Yes, I realized, that was a good idea.

Tom was part of a Kentuckian family that had a farm just east of town and was doing pretty well. He was a friendly and generous young man. He sometimes loaned Jim his white Plymouth convertible to take girls on dates.

Bob drove for Don Harbert, who owned a dairy farm. The equipment was far better than the trucks of the 1920s, but not always reliable. Bob recalled how once the headlights went out on his heavily loaded truck while he was driving down a steep, winding road into Madison, Indiana, an Ohio River port. He pulled out a flashlight and held it out the window to guide himself to the bottom, steering through the curves with one hand.

"Skip" Robbins, Curt Corn, Winifred "Wimp" Brunnemer, and his brother "Link" were among the other Whiteland entrepreneurs who went into trucking. They joked that their motto was "You call, we haul." But in the mid-1930s, politics caught up with Whiteland's truckers. Because long-haul truckers were faster and more versatile than the railroads in point-to-point carriage, they were cutting into the business of the rails, which had been federally regulated since 1887. Rail shipping rates had come under regulation because of complaints by shippers, mainly the politically powerful grain shippers of the West, that they were captive to the railroads because they had no other way of shipping. The railroads reached a modus vivendi with the Interstate Commerce Commission (ICC) that was reasonably comfortable for all concerned.

The Whiteland boys would ultimately have their initiative blunted by protectionist measures lobbied into federal law by their rail competitors. When in the 1930s modern trucks were undercutting the rails on price and service, the rails, also politically powerful, lobbied for and got the Motor Carrier Act of 1935, which brought truckers under the ICC's regulatory regime. It required truckers to get certificates of "public convenience and necessity" in order to operate.

Existing truckers who could prove their past service to shippers didn't have much trouble, and in a sense the law gave them some protection against competition as well. But it became very hard for a new trucker to break into the business. Soon the Whiteland truckers were painting ICC license numbers under "Coal and Grain" on the sides of their trucks. In return for being allowed to stay in the business they had to submit to ICC paperwork and rate making.

Shippers, of course, were also at the mercy of ICC rate making. The agency finally came under pressure for deregulatory change and was abolished in 1995. But not before becoming a poster boy for the governmental habit of favoring certain industries by protecting them from competition.

Proof that there were people in the United States who had made it big and were enjoying the good life even during the Depression could be found in the person of another colorful Whiteland character named Orel "Chewtabac" Woods, who earned the nickname with the chaw of tobacco usually socked in his jaw. Auto mechanics like Chew often chewed tobacco because it was dangerous to smoke cigarettes and cigars when you were working around gasoline engines. Chew was a mechanic and test driver for the Duesenberg Automobile & Motors Company in Indianapolis, and he drove a Duesenberg, or at least half of one, between his job and his Whiteland home.

Chew's test car didn't have a body. It was merely an engine, drive train, and chassis, on which was mounted a platform supporting a seat for the driver and a passenger, the steering wheel, and a control panel. Chew usually drove home for lunch. The powerful straight-eight Duesenberg engines that Chew tested had a tailpipe with a "cutout" to bypass the muffler. Chew could announce his arrival for lunch simply by switching to the cutout and giving full voice to that big engine.

We in Whiteland could hear him coming not long after he passed through Greenwood, four miles away. When he actually arrived the noise was deafening as he roared down Main Street in leather helmet and goggles to have a home-cooked lunch. Far from being annoyed, the townspeople loved the sound of that big straight eight, as well as all other breeds of that marvelous invention, the internal combustion engine, that had brought us such pleasure, privacy, and mobility.

Duesenberg was very big in Indy 500 racing in the 1920s and 1930s. The company, like other makers of stock cars then and now, used racing to advertise the superior engineering of their products. Chew was a hero around Whiteland because he had ridden as a mechanic in the Indy race. Riding mechanics were a feature of the race in those decades. They were sometimes given the fancy name "mechanicians" and it was their job to check for cars trying to pass, acting as a human rearview mirror, keeping an eye on tire wear and fuel supply and diagnosing any signs of a malfunction in either the engine or drive train. Chew also had driven on the track to test engines, but not in races.

Duesenberg succeeded in making its name as a builder of fine, and very expensive, cars partly through its successes at Indy. The company's race cars were frequent winners in the early days. In 1925, Pete DePaolo was the first driver to average more than 100 miles per hour for the five-hundred-mile race. He was driving a supercharged Duesenberg straight eight.

Every Duesenberg engine and chassis was tested before it was shipped to a coach designer to be customized for a high-rolling customer. Chew's testing job was proof that even in the middle of a depression there were Americans who were making enough money to afford a car costing six times what a Ford of that vintage would set you back. Movie stars like Gary Cooper were big fans of these high-priced, high-powered prestige cars and they are among the most treasured collector's items today. The only owner in Johnson County in the 1930s, so far as I know, was a Franklin doctor, William Province.

There was a lot going on around Whiteland. But still, residents sometimes got bored. Harry Porter once closed his drugstore, went to Indianapolis Airport, and hopped on an American Airlines DC-3 headed for San Francisco. What with a wife and four kids to support he didn't have enough money to stay long, but he saw the Golden Gate Bridge, and surveyed the city from Telegraph Hill. Then he boarded an eastbound flight and returned home. It was expensive, but it fulfilled a dream.

"Tack" Parkhurst, a lean bachelor with a large black mustache that gave him something of a Simon Legree look, once suffered the same pang. He lived in a run-down little house on the county road that paralleled the railroad tracks. The way locals pronounced Tack's last name sounded to me like "Parkas" and because of his exotic appearance I assumed he was of middle-European descent. But I would later learn that Tack was pretty much like the rest of us, who were mostly of Anglo-Saxon or Germanic origin, and was consequently less colorful than I had imagined in my youth. But colorful enough.

Tack was a chauffeur to Dr. David Phipps, better known as Old Doc Phipps, who was Whiteland's only doctor until young John Machledt set up shop in about 1940. Tack was something of a brooding presence, and there were tales that he sampled some of the mood-altering drugs on the doctor's medicine shelf. But surely Doc Phipps would not have willingly provided dope to a man who might be needed to drive him on gravel roads for a rural house call on a snowy night.

One summer Friday evening, Tack showed up at the barbershop and asked, "Who wants to go to St. Louis for a cup of coffee?" Although St. Louis was 250 miles away, and this was long before interstates, four town boys piled into Doc Phipps's big Buick. They rode all night, reaching St. Louis in the early dawn. They found a café open downtown, where they had a cup of coffee and some ham and eggs. Then they got back in the Buick and made the six-hour return trip to Whiteland. Such were the ways the men of our village conquered ennui.

Whiteland's most famous athletes in the 1930s came from a family of black sharecroppers who worked a farm east of town. Mortimer and Tommie Ann Crowe had ten children, two girls and eight boys, all superb athletes. Ray, the oldest boy, was a big scorer on the 1933–34 Whiteland basketball team. He became a track star at Indiana Central College in Indianapolis, now the University of Indianapolis. He was the basketball coach of Crispus Attucks, a mostly black high school in Indianapolis, when the team won two consecutive state tournaments in 1955 and 1956. Ray coached the great Oscar Robertson, who went on to fame in professional basketball.

Among other distinctions, including a stint in the Indiana state legislature, Ray appeared briefly in the 1986 movie *Hoo-*

siers as the coach of the team defeated by Gene Hackman's "Hickory" squad in the state finals at Butler Fieldhouse in Indianapolis. There was a legend around Whiteland that Ray had once hit a baseball all the way to the grain elevator. At a latter-day alumni banquet, I asked him if it was true. He replied, modestly, "Well, if you hit it up to the road it would have rolled all the way to the elevator." Of course, from there it would have been downhill. But hitting it up to the road would be a home run in most ballparks.

Ray once told an interviewer that he didn't feel any racial discrimination when he was growing up in Whiteland and it seems, looking back, that he was not only accepted but admired by his high school teammates, who included my brother Bob. His more famous younger brother, George, was not quite so lucky. After the Crowes gave up farming and moved to Franklin, George led Franklin High School in 1939 to the final game of the state basketball tournament. They failed to win the championship but he was clearly the outstanding player.

Trouble came when Franklin High scheduled a dinner to celebrate the team's achievement at Franklin's best restaurant, Snyder's. Al Snyder informed the school that his restaurant didn't admit blacks, so the banquet was held with the team's leading player absent, a scandal that at least served to raise the consciousness of fair-minded people in the county to the evils of racial discrimination. It caused a lot of rancor among basketball fans, which included just about everyone, and it certainly didn't do Al's reputation any good.

George played baseball in the Negro Leagues after World

War II, as well as professional basketball, teaming up with
Jackie Robinson, much more famous as a baseball player, of
course, on the 1947 Los Angeles Red Devils. It was only in
1952, when George was past thirty and nine years out of Indiana Central, that he was able to break into big-league baseball. His friend Jackie had broken the color barrier with the
Dodgers in 1947. But George made the most of it, playing for
nine years with National League teams. Filling in at first base
on the 1957 Cincinnati Reds for the injured Ted Kluszewski,
George hit thirty-one home runs. At one point he held the
record, since broken, for the most major-league pinch-hit
home runs, fourteen. Most folks in Whiteland were proud of
Ray and George, these two native sons.

CHAPTER FIFTEEN

★

BUT GIVE THE RAILROADS THEIR DUE

Railroads became protectionist in the 1930s, but those who built them had opened up the United States to settlement, commerce, and ease of travel in the nineteenth century. For a look at what they accomplished, search "U.S. Railways 1910" on Google and look at the incredible skein of railway lines in that year. They almost blacken the map. There were three ways to travel at the turn of the twentieth century: by foot, by horse or animal-drawn conveyance, or by rail. Motorcars were still experimental and most roadways were muddy tracks. Airplanes were mere engine-powered kites flown by daredevil aviators.

All that would change spectacularly in a short few decades, but in 1910 the railroads were king. They linked villages like Whiteland and Greenwood to the outside world. Indeed, they spawned the creation of such villages.

The Official Guide of the Railways for 1910 lists, by rough count, nearly five hundred railroad companies. It tells the reader the names of some seventy thousand stations, mostly serving what used to be called "jerkwater" towns, meaning small places where engine drivers stopped to refill their boilers with water. The guide lists the railroad or railroads serving each town. A traveler with enough time and patience in 1910 could board a train in Whiteland and travel just about anywhere, even to populated parts of Canada and Mexico. He could find his way to Waterville, Maine, or any of twelve other Watervilles in other states, or choose to go to Warrior, North Carolina; Warrior, Pennsylvania; or Warrior, Arizona. Few places were beyond his reach.

When James, Sara, and little Melba moved from Kentucky to Illinois, they packed up their sparse belongings and caught a Louisville & Nashville train in Munfordville, traveled to Louisville, caught a Wabash Line train from there to Chicago, and changed there to the Rock Island Line to go to Monmouth, Illinois. From there someone would have carried them by horse and wagon the short distance to the farm they were to work near the little town of Alexis. When they moved back to Louisville five years later it would have been by the same route.

By 1933, railroads had passed their prime as the favorite mode of transport for passengers, but even then, the Pennsylvania Railroad provided valuable services to little towns like Whiteland. Trains were still pulled by steam locomotives fueled with coal. The Pennsy's predecessor, the Jeffersonville, Indianapolis, & Madison, or JMI, had been Whiteland's lifeline to the outside world in the nineteenth century when the only other means of travel was by foot, horseback, or horse-drawn conveyance over primitive roads.

In the 1930s, passenger trains didn't stop at Whiteland anymore but they delivered the town's mail. Mildred Shinn, the postmistress, would put the outgoing mail in a bag made of leather and heavy canvas. Her husband, Harry, who worked for the railroad, would take it to a spot just north of the Railroad Street crossing and hang it on an ingenious device that dangled it near the train track. When the mail train sped by, a hook from the mail car would snag the bag and an attendant would haul it aboard. The crewman sorted it and mail from other towns en route to distribution centers in Louisville or Indianapolis.

The bag of mail coming to Whiteland was snagged by a similar device but it sometimes missed and the bag slid along the grassy berm. Harry picked up the mail and delivered it to his wife, who would sort it into the bank of numbered boxes for townspeople to pick up. Our number was 308.

Harry communicated with his railroad confreres by means of a telegraph terminal installed in a brick dispatcher's office on the south edge of town. From the windows of his elevated perch he had a good view of the track north and south. He controlled a semaphore signaling system that lowered a red paddle for stop and a green one if the track was clear. Before telephones, he had communicated by Morse code on a telegraph key. If he had a message for the train crew, he would post a looped hickory stick with message attached on a device

similar to the one used for mail so that the engineer or fire-
man could snag it on the fly as the train went by.

Fragile, heavy, or perishable items shipped by post sometimes required passenger trains to stop at the Whiteland depot.
Freight cars were spotted on the appropriate sidings by their
crews, a procedure interesting for small boys to observe. After
a brakeman disconnected the freight car to be spotted from the
remainder of the train, the engineer would back the free car onto
the siding and brake his engine with a quick chuffing sound
and a cloud of steam from the steam vent. A brakeman riding
the coasting car would stop it at the desired spot, usually within
reach of the elevator's loading spout. Freight cars were spotted on
another siding adjacent to Stokely's for unloading cans from the
American Can Company plant in Cincinnati or packing cases
from Inland Container Corporation in Indianapolis. The outgoing shipments were cases of Stokely canned products.

Passenger trains were a reminder for small-town folks of the larger culture of which they were a part. The cars had colorful names, like "Appalachian Waterfall," lettered on their sides, evoking thoughts of distant places one should certainly someday visit, by train of course.

One summer day at sundown, I was riding my bicycle home from an errand and found my way blocked by an express train that had stopped to await a green signal from Harry Shinn's semaphore. The dining car was positioned in front of me, and in the rays of the setting sun, I could see well-dressed people living the good life inside. Such a scene would years later be described by Johnny Cash in his "Folsom Prison Blues," which imagined a train dining car with people "drinkin' coffee and smoking big cigars."

My people were dining at tables with white tablecloths, being served by black waiters in white coats carrying food in silver Thermadors. Their tables were lit romantically with white candles. A pretty woman in a yellow dress smiled and waved to the goggle-eyed urchin leaning on the handlebars of his bicycle, me. I embarrassedly waved back, feeling that I was being teased just a little bit but finding it not unpleasant.

The diners had to be well-off, because dining car meals were expensive. Did I want to be like them, sitting in a dining car looking out at the people of a country village during a brief stop on a journey to somewhere far more glamorous? Well, it would mean staying dressed up a lot. But yes, I guess so. I doubt that I was alone in that desire among the other Whitelanders waiting for this elegant, sunlit scene to move on down the line. As with the glamour we saw in movies, it inspired us.

CHAPTER SIXTEEN

★

A NATION OF SHOPKEEPERS

PRESIDENT CALVIN COOLIDGE has been mocked by urban sophisticates over the years for saying the business of America is business. They have scoffed that America is about a lot more than the humdrum practice of buying and selling. It's about art, literature, music, and much else. Or what about labor unions, universities, nongovernment institutions, and, of course, government? They are right, of course, but also miss Coolidge's point. He was talking about the American economy of that era, or in other words about the rather important matter of earning a living.

What Coolidge actually said in 1925 to a Washington,

D.C., gathering of the American Society of Newspaper Editors contained, in the context of that ninety-years-ago stage of American history, about as much truth as you are ever likely to get from a politician.

He said: "After all, the chief business of the American people is business. They are profoundly concerned with producing, buying, selling, investing and prospering in the world. I am strongly of the opinion that the great majority of people will always find these the moving impulses of life."

Coolidge made those comments when a far higher proportion of American workers than today ran their own businesses rather than working for government or big corporations. As Napoleon Bonaparte once said contemptuously of the British, we were "a nation of shopkeepers," in both the cities and towns.

In the towns like Whiteland and Franklin, the shopkeepers were adjunct to that other form of small business, the family farm. Small business and the "family farm" are still extolled in politics today even though farms have grown much larger and often have been corporatized, and shops are often part of large-scale retail or franchise chains manned mostly by hired hands, not the owners. The Small Business Administration and the Department of Agriculture still enjoy substantial political support today even though the raison d'être for the assistance they provide is largely a matter of the past, if it ever existed at all. Efforts to preserve the small economic institutions of a long-gone era have proved to be mostly unsuccessful.

But in 1933, a decade after Coolidge's remarks, America was still a place where small retail and farm businesses were the economic bedrock. Whiteland was an exemplar of that. It was a distinct and clearly defined community. Folks there knew who they were and felt no embarrassment at all about their identities as residents of a small farm village. After all, they had plenty of company across the United States.

Everywhere you looked, people were running businesses. We had only one doctor and no lawyers. There were no Walmarts, Home Depots, or Burger Kings. But we had our general stores, a small café that could provide hot dogs and hamburgers to go with your coffee or Coke, a barbershop, a blacksmith, an auto repair shop, and a cobbler. There were places where you could fill up the tank of your car or truck with gasoline. We were the center of Pleasant Township, a landscape of small farms. The only governmental presence was a small post office, with a single postmistress and one rural mail carrier, hardly a government bureaucracy. If you needed a product or service, within the limits of the kinds of needs we had, you could usually find it in Whiteland. A good many people didn't own cars, because they didn't have need for one. And of course, not many years before, no one owned cars, because they didn't exist.

We were comparable to Garrison Keillor's fictional Minnesota town of Lake Wobegon, "where all the women are strong, all the men are good-looking and all the children are above average." Actually, our IQs and literacy levels might have been a bit above average for the country at large. Running a business, particularly a farm, was demanding in an era when money was tight and there was little room for error. The incomes and even the business survival of farmers were dependent on correctly judging what to plant, how to balance the cost of planting against the likely return, and evaluating variables like weather, markets, and government policies. Mistakes could be costly, as my father once learned, and the narrow returns didn't leave much margin for error. Farmers and farm town tradesmen developed a certain canniness in the arts of producing, buying, and selling that President Coolidge extolled.

Bob once worked for an imaginative entrepreneur named Charles S. Stoner, who ran a filling station three miles north of town on U.S. 31. Stoner had saved enough money for this new business by working as a rag picker, touring the countryside in a truck buying up worn-out clothing to sell to rug makers, in particular the makers of hooked rugs, those inexpensive circular braided floor coverings popular in the 1930s. He also bought scrap metal to sell to Indianapolis dealers, an important component of steel making then as now.

Nothing much was wasted in the 1930s, not because of recycling drives, but because everything had some value. I remember Pat Good, of Stokely, selling some worn-out brass colanders used for processing tomato juice to a scrap dealer. Pat insisted that a worker smash them with sledgehammers so the dealer couldn't resell them as still viable. The dealer was affronted by this show of distrust.

But back to Stoner. To make a little extra money at the filling station he got the idea of harvesting sassafras roots in the forests of Brown County, in those same hills where Connie once scouted for illicit mountain dew. The procedure was to peel off the root bark and package it in glassine bags to sell to customers who might have a fancy for sassafras tea. A piece of bark steeped in boiling water made a reddish-looking beverage that was said to be good for what ailed you, a pungent and refreshing tonic. It was a nice sideline product for Stoner's filling station, earning him fifteen cents a bag and costing him little except the bags and Bob's labor.

The drawback, at least from the Melloan family's point of view, was that Bob would come home from work reeking of sass-afras. His work clothes collected the orange-red dust of the product so he bore some resemblance to a Tibetan monk, except that he was not wearing a robe.

I have for years marveled at Stoner's imagination, so typical of the insouciance with which so many Americans faced the ravages of depression and, later, war. In addition to his fuel and sassafras business, Stoner operated behind his station what came to be known as Stoner's field. There he had a small racetrack, where he staged novel competitions. One was "pushmobile" races that featured small race cars put together by local mechanics, driven by third-grade boys, and pushed by means of a pole by local athletes.

My friend Wayne McIntire won almost every race. His garageman father, Jack, in a labor of love, had crafted what looked like a miniature Indy car, with balloon tires and excellent steering. More important, Wayne had the best pushers. They included the aforementioned Ray Crowe, the Central Normal track star, as part of a five-man relay team. Wayne and his pushers in 1933 also won a street race in Greenwood sponsored by local businessmen. The prize was eighteen dollars, not a princely sum even at that time when shared by the team, but nonetheless a nice token of victory.

Stoner also held goat-cart races with little girls as the drivers. The goats and carts were supplied by a Indianapolis area farmer-entrepreneur name Edison Lucas. In one race a man in the audience shouted to one of the drivers, "Twist her tail, Annabale!" She did and won. Stoner and Lucas no doubt made some money out of the races, Stoner mainly by selling soft drinks and candy. There was no bonanza to be found in this kind of entertainment in the 1930s. But I would guess that it pleased Stoner to know that he was supplying his neighbors with enjoyable recreation.

CHAPTER SEVENTEEN

★

MAKING FOOD LAST

The Dunn Farm

As with most small towns and cities of the era, Whiteland's main industry was food production, processing, and preservation. One of the great inventions of modern times was the preservation of food by canning. Learning how to do this was a recent development historically, dating back only to the early nineteenth century. It was then that factories were created in both England and New York to seal food in tin cans.

The inventors were not sure initially why vacuum sealing worked to prevent rot, and it was learned only a half century later, thanks to the microbial research of Louis Pasteur, that sealing denied the microorganisms that caused food to spoil the air they needed to breathe. Canning meant that the surplus production of farmers in the growing months could be stored and sold later, adding greatly to the value of crops and eliminating much of the waste and sickness caused by food spoilage.

The Mason glass jar was invented in 1858 by John Landis Mason, a Philadelphia tinsmith, as an alternative to tin cans that made household canning practical. Not long thereafter the factories of the five Ball brothers in Muncie, Indiana, were flooding the nation with Ball Mason jars, which had screw-on or fliptop caps with a rubber sealing gasket that made home canning easy. It didn't take any central planners to tell farmers that this was a great thing, an invention that allowed farm families to lay down canned food in the summer and fall to sustain themselves through the winter until the next crop.

And no one had to tell would-be entrepreneurs that it would be a good business to start canning factories. In the late nineteenth century, Laura Polk and James T. Polk of Greenwood began a small-scale canning enterprise in their kitchen. Laura "canned" tomatoes from nearby gardens in Mason jars and James hauled them by horse and wagon to Indianapolis to sell. Among his customers were restaurant owners and hotel chefs. It was such a good business that the Polks set up a larger-scale operation in their barn. And when that proved too small to meet demand, they built factories, not only to can the tomatoes but to produce their own tin cans as a replacement for jars.

By 1887, Polk Canning Company was a big operation, employing 500 people and contracting with 150 farmers to supply tomatoes. To ensure a steady supply of labor the Polks built a dormitory to house the young women who came from other towns and distant farms to work in their factory, peeling tomatoes and filling cans and bottles.

Sophisticates of a later era might scoff at such arrangements as representative of the paternalism displayed by tycoons at the turn of the nineteenth and into the twentieth century. Tennessee Ernie Ford's line in the song "Sixteen Tons" comes to mind: "I owe my soul to the company store." Certainly, some companies took pains to hold workforces captive to company housing and company stores. But quite a few also wanted to ensure that their employees had decent living conditions. At the very least, they understood that measures to keep workers healthy and in good spirits would serve the company's interests as well.

My guess is that Mr. and Mrs. Polk, considering their other good works for the community, had parental feelings about the young women they housed in their dormitories. Judging from the behavioral rules they laid down, they wanted to protect not only the health of these girls but also their virtue, a possession perhaps more prized then than it is today, although that might be highly debatable.

The Polks also sought to maximize efficiency. Rather than let the peelings and other by-products of the canning process go to waste, they turned some of it into cattle feed, acquired a herd of Holsteins and started a dairy, bottling "Polk's Best" milk and delivering it to stores and homes, initially by horse-drawn vans and later by trucks. J. T. Polk Company became Greenwood's largest industry and the Polks among the largest benefactors to the Greenwood community, building a community house and supporting other civic improvements.

Canning factories sprang up this way all over the nation where arable land was available for diversified farming. Farm-to-market road building and the presence of these factories provided the vital link between the farmers' fields and the dining room tables of urban consumers. The factories were invariably built with access to railroads, so their products could be cased and shipped by freight car to distant markets, finding their way into the small mom-and-pop groceries that were the mainstay of food retailing in the centuries before the advent of self-service supermarkets in the mid-twentieth century.

Whiteland-area farms in the early twentieth century were highly diversified, as were most family farms throughout the land. Farmers husbanded livestock and grew several "cash" crops to supply themselves with dollar income. The soil around Johnson County, and indeed much of Indiana, was rich enough to grow tomatoes, one of the more valuable cash crops. In the 1910s and '20s, Whiteland farmers along with hired help would pick tomatoes, load them into hampers supplied by the factory, stack the hampers onto a farm wagon, and drive the team of horses pulling the wagon a few miles on graveled roads to the Whiteland canning factory. There the tomatoes would be canned whole or made into catsup or chili sauce, packed into cases, and loaded onto a freight car at the factory loading dock. A train would transport the cases to wholesale warehouses in cities like Indianapolis, Chicago, or Louisville, from where other horses and wagons would distribute them to grocers serving local neighborhoods.

No central authority planned this highly efficient production and distribution system. It was user-created. Successful economies are built from the ground up, not the top down. The system was the creation of individual entrepreneurs seeing needs and opportunities and solving any problems, like inadequate roads, that stood in the way of making the system work. This sort of thing was happening all over America in the late nineteenth and early twentieth centuries as enterprising individuals like the Polks created the basic industrial and distributional infrastructure that their successors would develop further into the modern economy of today. Farmers were still delivering tomatoes to the Whiteland canning factory by horse and wagon well into the 1930s, although each year there would be more trucks and fewer wagons.

One of the early owners of the Whiteland canning factory was another Greenwood capitalist, Grafton Johnson, an eccentric banker known for his hobby of boarding wild animals. In the 1920s, he kept lions and bears on his fenced estate on the south edge of Greenwood. The lions were caged but bears had freer rein and would sometimes climb over the fence to visit downtown Greenwood, throwing the community into a bit of a panic. Since Grafton was the richest man in town, a millionaire, so it was said, the police were deferential toward his eccentricities.

The Stokely brothers, James and John, along with their widowed mother, Anna, started their canning business in Cocke County, Tennessee, in 1898, packing the produce from their farm, loading it onto boats on the French Broad River, and shipping it to Knoxville and Chattanooga. They were later joined by brothers William, George, and Jehu and the family launched an aggressive expansion mainly through mergers and acquisitions, creating their own labels and fashioning a national distribution system for a range of Stokely brands. In the 1920s, the Stokelys bought the Polk canning business in Greenwood and the Whiteland factory. By 1941, they operated thirty-four factories in fourteen states.

Other canning factory operators in Johnson County were less expansive. Morgan Packing Company of Austin, Indiana, started in 1899, eventually had eight plants in Indiana, including one in Franklin. They had their own brands but also packed house brands for distributors. The other packing plant in Franklin in the 1920s and '30s was locally owned and operated by the Hougland family.

Managers of the canning companies would estimate their sales prospects and check their inventories in late winter and decide how much of each product they wanted to can. Then their field agents would meet with farmers and accept offers to supply what the factory needed. The agent would write contracts with each farmer, setting the price to be paid and how much acreage the farmer would allot for each product.

Arrangements were made for the factory to ship farmers seed of the required quality, or in the case of tomatoes, plants started in the early spring in warmer climates like southern

Georgia and Arkansas. The tomato plants for Whiteland farmers would arrive by rail at the Whiteland depot at planting time in June, packed in trapezoidal wooden crates and kept moist by wet Spanish moss from the oak trees of the South to keep them fresh. Farmers would load them onto their trucks or wagons and take them immediately to the fields for planting.

The factories in Johnson County in the early 1930s packed a variety of products besides tomatoes, including sweet corn, beets, and green beans. Stokely's in Whiteland began the canning season in June by receiving peas, hauled in by farmers, vine and all, to be put through big machines called pea viners at the factory and then shelled from the pods by local women. Sadie Henry, a quick, wiry woman, was one of the fastest shellers, and generous as well. Once when Sis was working summers on the shelling line, Sadie recognized that she was not especially nimble with her fingers and dumped some of her peas in Sis's bucket, a kind gesture Sis never forgot.

All four canning factories in Greenwood, Whiteland, and Franklin made it through the Depression, providing jobs for locals and migrants and income for their suppliers, the local farmers. An insight into the Hougland operation is provided by a legal brief the company filed on May 28, 1957, with the U.S. Tax Court in Indianapolis, trying to get relief from the World War II–vintage federal "excess profits" tax.

The Houglands claimed, quite logically, that the base years for the tax included the abnormally low profits earned during the deepest Depression years, and thus lowered the threshold for what would be considered excess profits. In terms of fairness they had a point. Indeed the entire concept of "ex-cess" profits, conceived in Washington ostensibly to prevent "war profiteering," had some serious definitional problems, including the one identified by the Houglands, using lean Depression year profits or losses to calculate the averages for what was considered "normal." But the court wasn't about to unloose an avalanche of similar claims, so it denied the petition. This economically unsound tax was belatedly repealed at the end of the Korean War in 1953.

The papers show how the Hougland family, headed by Daniel M. "Matt" Hougland, made out packing mostly corn and tomato products during the Depression. Their records reveal that during those years they cut back sharply on the amount of acreage they reserved, reductions that along with the reduced prices they paid of course lowered the income of their farmer suppliers. In their lowest profit years, 1931, 1932, 1938, and 1939, the company earned an average of only $3,540 annually, despite cuts in the salaries of the five owner-operators. In their highest years, 1924, 1928, 1934, and 1935, they averaged $95,078.

They suffered net losses of $16,379 in 1931 and $8,098 in 1932, recovering, interestingly enough, with net profits of $38,989 in 1933 and $76,640 in 1934 as the U.S. economy began to pull out of the depths of the "first depression." Things went smoothly until the "second depression" hit the country in 1937. They would suffer another loss, although a small one of only $954, in 1938, and a poor return in 1939. After that, it was onward and upward again into the war years of "excess profits."

The 1930s were a time when business taxes and regulation were smaller fixed expenses than now, so companies could adapt to changing markets more easily. The annual taxes of Hougland Packing amounted to less than $2,000 in the bad years, although if you compare that to their average earnings, it's not nothing.

Farmers were hit harder than the factories. In 1932, the average price paid to Indiana farmers dropped to $7.20 a ton for sweet corn in the husk, down from $13.20 in 1930. One of Hougland's sweet corn suppliers was Roy Sharp, whose 210-acre farm produced a variety of crops and boarded hogs, beef cattle, and a dairy herd. Sweet corn was one of Roy's cash crops, earning some of the money he needed to run the farm and support his wife, two daughters, and three sons. He must have wondered whether growing sweet corn was worth the effort when he sold his output to Hougland's in 1932.

Assuming Roy was getting the average market price, a truckload of sweet corn delivered to the Hougland dock in Franklin fetched less than $15. According to the Conference Board, a private research organization, the average weekly pay of an unskilled nonfarm worker in May–June 1932 was $15.33. Assuming that Roy had planted 30 acres in sweet corn and harvested 25 truckloads at the average per-acre yield in Indiana in those days, his entire crop would have brought only $245 before deducting expenses.

That was a slim reward for all the work he and his sons had done. Preparing the land in the spring involved harnessing his team of horses, hitching them to a gang plow to turn the soil, then switching to another tool with an array of bladed disks to pulverize the clods. After that he would go over the land again with his horses pulling a wooden platform called a "drag" to smooth the soil and yet again with a heavy steel cylinder called a "roller" to compact the smoothed earth. Only then would he hitch his horses to his corn planter, a machine that dispensed seed corn from two containers through tubes extending to blades that created furrows for the seeds and closed the furrow after they dropped.

When the new cornstalks were knee-high, he drove through the field again with a cultivator, a machine equipped with an array of hoes, to take out the weeds that would otherwise stunt the corn's growth. And finally he and his sons would drive down the rows, break off the ears of corn, and throw them into their truck to haul to Hougland's five miles away. They did all this for a truckload equivalent in value to one week's wage that an unskilled factory worker might earn, which itself was a meager reward.

But Roy's family had some distinct advantages over a factory worker. The factory worker in 1932–33 had faced a large risk of not having any income at all, because he might be one of the roughly 25 percent of workers who didn't have a job. Further, Roy, like other Whiteland area farmers, was diversified. He grew feed corn for calves he bought to fatten into full-sized beeves to sell at the Indianapolis stockyards. He and his sons milked twelve dairy cows twice a day, pouring the milk into eight-gallon cans that were placed on a roadside platform to be picked up and hauled by truck to Polk's dairy in Greenwood. He grew wheat for flour and tomatoes and pumpkins.

Some Whiteland area farmers went even further afield in diversification. Jim Davis, who had a small tomato farm on the south edge of Whiteland, kept beehives and sold the honey locally. He also raised tobacco, an unusual crop for Indiana, and dried it in his own tobacco barn.

Mary Carolyn Wendt, one of Roy Sharp's two daughters, said that her father was adept at switching to crops that had the best market possibilities and also at getting the most out of his land. He planted pumpkin seeds with his feed corn seeds, so that in the fall there would be both pumpkins and corn to harvest from the same field. He would then get a third crop from the field by running a one-horse wheat drill between the rows of mature feed corn in the fall to sow winter wheat, which would come up in the spring. When she was a little girl Carolyn would run ahead of the horse-drawn wheat drill to move pumpkins out of the way.

★

CHAPTER EIGHTEEN

THE HUCKSTERS

The Sharps

THE SHARPS, LIKE other farmers, had security during hard times not available to nonfarmers. They could live off the land. Whereas an unemployed factory worker in the city might have to seek relief from a soup kitchen, the Salvation Army, or a government agency, the Sharp family could subsist quite comfortably on a small portion of what their farm produced. Carolyn describes how they lived:

"If it wasn't raised in the garden, we didn't have it to eat. Mother canned fruits and vegetables. A hog was butchered every year, as well as a beef. [Butchering was often a group effort of several farmers, much like the threshing rings.] The pork that was cured, hams, and bacon hung in what we called the smokehouse. The rest of the pork was cooked in some fashion, generally fried, then placed in tin cans. We had a sealer and when finished they looked like commercially prepared cans. Then they were placed in boilers, covered with water, and placed on the coal range, where the water kept boiling. It was hours, not minutes, that they cooked. I never knew any that spoiled. The grease 'rendered' from cooking meat would harden into lard and would be stored for later cooking use in large five-gallon lard cans.

"Mother would cut bacon off the side of pork that had been cured. After a period of time it was possible there would be mold. She cut the mold off and still used the bacon. We often remarked in later years that we got our penicillin early." (Penicillin, made from a mold, wasn't produced commercially until World War II. Also during World War II, housewives were urged to donate their bacon fat to the government. The glycerin extracted from it was used to make bombs and munitions.)

Garden produce was also preserved, writes Carolyn. "Sweet potatoes were dug, wrapped individually in paper, and stored in an upstairs closet that was not heated. Irish potatoes were dug and stored in the cellar. We ate well."

Carolyn's mother, Marguerite, like mine after we moved to

town, would order baby chicks by mail, I'm not sure from what hatchery but probably one not very distant. One morning every spring you could walk into the Whiteland post office and hear a great deal of cheeping. The chicks had arrived! They came by express trains—that made special stops to unload them—in what looked like suit boxes, but divided into four compartments so the chicks wouldn't bunch up and smother each other.

The owners would claim them, bring them home to a chicken wire enclosure, and put them in an incubator, which was a hooded shelter with a heater fueled by coal oil, with trays for water and chicken feed. There they would mature, grow feathers, be turned out into the chicken yard, and eventually become family Sunday dinners or egg producers.

As Carolyn puts it: "As the chickens grew it became evident which were pullets (female) and which were roosters. The roosters were the ones we ate. In due time, the pullets were moved to the henhouse, where there would be nests for them to lay their eggs and roosts for them to perch at night. Eggs were gathered every day. What we didn't eat were placed in a crate and taken every week to the Greenwood creamery that also supplied stores with eggs. With the money from the eggs, Mother would purchase what she needed at the grocery."

Sometimes the groceries came to the farmers. The "huckster wagon" that visited the Melloan farm came from Russell Rund's grocery on State Highway 135. These grocery stores on wheels, dating back to when farm families were more limited in their ability to get into town, had regular routes through the countryside.

As Carolyn writes, "You didn't have to flag them down.

They just stopped. Mother would have eggs for them that she bartered for something she needed. Sometimes she would give my sister and me an egg and we could get a piece of candy. The huckster also had chicken coops on the back of the truck and mother often would sell chickens or hens for cash."

Of course, one requirement for being able to subsist with what a farm produces is being able to hang on to the farm. The Sharp family, like a great many others, was not entirely secure in that respect. And the federal farm banks were not always benign. Mary Carolyn remembers that when she was a six-year-old in 1933, two men in suits came to the farm. They were from the Federal Land Bank in Louisville, one of the twelve farm loan banks set up by the Wilson administration in 1916 to provide cheaper credit for farmers.

We farm children of that era were always wary of men in suits, unless it was Sunday, because they were usually bankers or someone else who spelled trouble. Carolyn eavesdropped on their conversation with her father. She didn't understand much but she remembers hearing the word *foreclosure*. Fortunately, Roy persuaded them to cut him some slack, allowing him to pay only interest on his mortgage until times improved, and the Sharps remained on their farm until Roy and Marguerite retired.

Joan Minner of Franklin (whom I would later marry) recalled another such experience when she was a child of about the same age. She looked out the window of the family's farmhouse to see Mary and Harry, her mother and father, standing by the cherry tree in the yard talking quietly. Her father was weeping, something she had never seen before. The family was living and working on a sizable farm owned by Harry's father, George Minner. George was descended from Germans Ernst and Frederika Minner, who had come to Johnson County from the Thuringian town of Koenigsee in 1851 and were among the early settlers of the farmland outside Franklin.

The Minners' bankers in Franklin had just told Harry's parents that they would extend the mortgage on the farm only on condition that they turn over the farm's operation to their son. Harry had had advanced training in modern farming techniques at Purdue University and his youth was no doubt a factor in the bank's demand.

Harry's parents had refused, which was why he was crying in anger and frustration. Apparently a rift had developed some years earlier over Harry's refusal to follow his parents' wishes that he marry a farm girl who would be heir to more land. Instead he had eloped with Mary Rust, a pretty and accomplished schoolteacher in Franklin.

As Harry could foresee from the way things were going, the elder Minners would later lose their farm to a smooth-talking fraudster who called himself Colonel McCord. Harry's sister Blanche, the widow of yet another farmer, would lose her land as well to the same charlatan. Blanche hanged herself with a rope tied to the rafters in her garage. Harry, Mary and their three children had a tough time. At one point Harry would have to go on "relief," taking a job with the Works Progress Administration (WPA) on a road gang. But they survived.

CHAPTER NINETEEN

FDR LOCKS UP SAVINGS

Wᴇ ʜᴀᴅ ᴍᴏᴠᴇᴅ into town at a time when the New Deal was addressing banking problems in a dramatic fashion. After taking office in March 1933, President Roosevelt responded to a string of bank failures by declaring a "bank holiday." It was hardly a joyous holiday. To forestall runs on banks, his decree limited how much Americans could withdraw from their accounts in national banks until the banks could be examined and certified sound. Some states had taken such actions, with regard to state banks, even earlier.

A month earlier, even before FDR's decree, the *Franklin Evening Star* reported that Johnson County banks, in accordance with a decision by the Indianapolis Clearing House Association, were limiting withdrawals to an amount not greater than 5 percent of total deposits. Clearinghouses were a holdover from the pre–Federal Reserve days, when banks essentially regulated themselves, but they were still a mechanism for coordinated activity by banks and their regulators.

Gilding the lily, the *Star* wrote that "not only was there no criticism from local banks for the unexpected action but on the other hand there was praise for the quick decision to limit withdrawals just as soon as it was learned of the action of the Indianapolis banks, where Johnson County banks carry practically all of their surplus funds. It was the only action that could have been taken, in fairness to all depositors, was the general verdict."

One wonders if this remarkable sanguinity also applied to depositors not able to get their money out of the bank as the national freeze was imposed and dragged on. Presumably not. Depositors of the Whiteland National Bank, which earlier in the year, under direction from the U.S. comptroller of the currency, had been merged with two Franklin banks into a new Johnson County National Bank, were not made whole until nine months later and even then, not entirely. It was only in December that they were able to recover a penultimate 30 percent that left only 5 percent frozen.

The ever-cheerful *Star* wrote of this as a joyful occasion. How joyful was it for depositors to not have access to their money for nine months, one must wonder. Maybe the *Star's* determination to spread joy was itself a reflection of the seriousness of the crisis. The paper's editors knew that runs on banks by depositors clamoring for their money could be scary. So they didn't seem to mind draconian government measures to prevent such panics, no matter what the implications might be for the sanctity of private property and the chances for economic recovery.

Nationally, the freeze on bank deposits that began with FDR's "bank holiday" ended within a reasonable time for many banks after it was determined that they were sufficiently capitalized. But for others it dragged on as federal examiners pored over the quality of bank assets relative to their capital and borrowings and merged some with stronger institutions as a condition of reopening. This process took time, and during that time a lot of money was frozen, contributing to what was already a shortage of money—deflation, in other words. It was only at the beginning of September that the comptroller of the currency was able to announce a thaw, saying that "in several weeks" only 6 percent of bank deposits would be locked up.

But during the first half of 1933, deposits of national banks had dropped by $1.7 billion and loans had dropped accordingly, falling by 17 percent in six months. By June 30, there were 4,902 licensed national banks, versus 7,506 in October 1929. The surviving banks were about the same number that had existed in 1914, but they were supported by 70 percent more capital.

The bank holiday and its immediate aftermath raised the

question still debated by monetary economists of whether the holiday itself weakened the incipient 1933 recovery by tying up the savings of many depositors for an extended period of time. It also has occurred to some economists that the Federal Reserve System, created in 1913 to ensure against bank runs by extending emergency loans to banks, seemed to have been missing in action when it was really needed.

Indeed, the creation of the Fed hadn't prevented bank failures. There had been a whole string of them in the 1920s, despite the aid available from the Fed. What was being demonstrated in the early 1930s was that the Fed was not very effective in stabilizing banking and probably contributed to the problem through its failure to effectively address the rapid deflation caused by the 1929 crash.

The question still debated is whether FDR was justified in shutting down the entire federal banking system for what for some depositors would be months, thereby crippling the conduct of normal business activity in places like Franklin, Greenwood, and Whiteland. Was the banking system in that much danger from runs, or would weak banks have been winnowed out naturally, as they eventually were by the decrees of examiners? Certainly it didn't help matters when FDR gave angry speeches to the nation excoriating "money changers" for problems that were at base caused by government itself.

The other drastic FDR measure was to take the United States off what was left of the gold standard. In 1933, Congress nullified the public's right to demand gold in the payment of a debt. New legislation also required holders of monetary gold or gold certificates to turn in their gold to the nearest Federal

Reserve bank. They would receive in return Federal Reserve notes, that is, dollars, at the long-standing gold standard rate of $20.67 an ounce. After the Fed's vaults were stocked with vast amounts of confiscated gold, FDR in 1934 raised the fiat price of gold to $35.

Although the gold measures made it illegal in the United States for private citizens to use gold as money, the Fed still exchanged the yellow metal with other central banks to settle trade balances. Thus the 66 percent increase in the price that FDR decreed was, in effect, a devaluation of the dollar relative to other currencies. It was intended to "reflate" the dollar by reducing its purchasing power and thereby end deflation.

It worked to a degree, but not dramatically. As James Grant not long ago noted in his *Interest Rate Observer* newsletter, consumer prices edged up 0.8 percent in 1933 but never climbed at an annual rate above 3 percent throughout the 1930s, despite all the federal efforts, some ruled unconstitutional by the Supreme Court, to force prices upward. Of course, even inflation below 3 percent was hardly welcomed by consumers, in that it mainly reflected a cheapening of money, not an increase in the value of the products they were scraping up money to buy.

Nonetheless, the economy was starting a weak pickup cycle in 1933 and the New Deal would claim credit for that thereafter, either legitimately or illegitimately, take your choice. The New Deal's Banking Act of 1933 did have some arguably salutary provisions. It created the Federal Deposit Insurance Corporation (FDIC), insuring deposits at member banks up to $250,000, initially funded by premiums from the banks but with implicit government backing. Some purists have argued that deposit insurance encouraged bankers to take greater risks, referred to by economists as "moral hazard." But on the whole it seemed to have restored the confidence of small depositors and reduced the impulse to withdraw savings at any sign of trouble.

More problematical, the 1933 act separated deposit-taking lending institutions making commercial loans from "investment" banks involved in presumably riskier securities trading and underwriting ventures. Some would argue that this so-called Glass-Steagall provision of the 1933 act was punishment for a crime banks hadn't committed: pumping up the prices of stocks and paving the way for the 1929 crash. Banks did in fact finance speculation, but it can be argued that there were many other reasons for the crash, especially the ending of the 1920s credit boom and the tendency of stock prices to fall during a downturn in the business cycle. Yet there was some merit in separating insured depository institutions from what is arguably the more volatile investment banking. That argument was reawakened after the 2008 crash, with calls for bringing back Glass-Steagall, which had gone by the boards in the 1990s.

For whatever reasons, banking became more stable after the 1933 act and the end of the disruptive bank holiday. The New Deal framers of the 1933 Banking Act deserve credit for that. That's not to say that the dollar itself was stable or that the Fed's management of monetary policy was put on a sounder footing, as the crash of 1937 would demonstrate.

★

CHAPTER TWENTY

FARMING FIATS

Bᴜᴛ ʙᴀᴄᴋ ᴛᴏ the farm bill, which would have lasting effects on farm communities like Whiteland. The Agricultural Adjustment Act of 1933 was arguably the most dubious of the New Deal's legacies. The AAA was a remarkable document in the extent to which it empowered the federal government to reach into the lives and work of the nation's farmers and dictate how much they could produce, through measures justified by their authors as a rescue mission. Unmentioned was that they were being rescued from other government policies, principally Smoot-Hawley and a Federal Reserve Board not up to the job of stabilizing the value of the currency.

Of course, central planners like Secretary of Agriculture Henry Wallace and brain truster Rexford Tugwell were not entirely to blame for this. The farm lobbies were demanding higher prices and the New Dealers were trying to figure out ways, however intrusive and often wacky, to give them what they wanted.

When the Agricultural Adjustment Act of 1933 attempted to respond to this demand by restricting production through acreage allotments and other intrusive measures, not all farmers agreed with their lobbyists. But it's not unusual for a powerful lobby to acquire a life of its own and make claims exaggerating how many members of the organization it represents actually agree with its positions. A good modern example would be AARP Inc., which runs both a nonprofit organization of retired persons and a big business providing its endorsements of a wide range of products, including supplemental health insurance, car rentals, cruises, and lodging. Many of its members sign up to get discounts on these products. And a great many disagree with AARP's lobbying positions, as evidenced by the number who dropped out after it backed President Obama's Affordable Care Act, better known as Obamacare.

Labor union lobbyists in Washington and statehouses make similar claims, even when closed-shop requirements force workers who disagree with their political position to pay union dues. The 1988 U.S. Supreme Court ruling in *Communications Workers of America v. Beck* attempted to remedy this by holding that union members can demand refunds of that portion of their dues used for political purposes, but it's not evident that *Beck* in practice has led to much restraint on union lobbying for policies that some of their members don't favor.

On August 18, 1933, an editorial in the *Greenwood News,* a Democrat weekly, let area farmers know what to expect from the new agriculture act. Because of the national wheat surplus, wheat growers in Johnson County would be restricted to an allotment of 314,585 bushels for the crop year 1934. The applications of individual farmers to the U.S. Department of Agriculture (USDA) for their federally allotted production quotas would have certain requirements. They must list how many bushels were harvested in 1930, 1931, and 1932 and state how the crops were disposed of. There must be a certificate of the threshing machine operator certifying how much wheat was gleaned in those years. A sketch map of the farm must be included. All this must be certified by a township committee authorized by the USDA to make the final determination of how much wheat each farmer could grow in 1934.

In a requirement suggestive of the methods of the old Soviet Union, whose organizational methods had impressed AAA designer Tugwell during his visit in 1928, the farmers were encouraged to spy on each other. "Neighbors will study each farmer's allotment to compare to their knowledge of wheat previously produced. Allotments too high will be questioned by neighboring farmers." In other words, the cooperative, collegial spirit of the farmers in the threshing rings would now become spiteful tattling to help the government enforce quotas.

The allotment applications would be forwarded to Washington and if approved the farmer would receive a 20-cent government subsidy on each bushel of wheat produced and another 8 cents a bushel if his actual yield stayed within his allotment.

Syndicated newspaper columnist Arthur Brisbane described the AAA as the most radical departure from established farming methods in the history of agriculture. That description probably pleased Tugwell and his fellow brain trusters. The Sharp family, when they looked at the coercive measures in the act, didn't find the prospect of regimented farming quite so pleasing, according to Mary Carolyn.

New Deal propagandists claimed that their programs were designed to save the small family farms, much beloved by farm state politicians if one could believe their speeches. In fact, the farm bill measures probably hastened the demise of small farms. For one thing, the production quotas idled a great deal of farmland of small producers, rendering their farms unprofitable even with subsidies. Moreover, subsidies were paid to farm owners, not tenant farmers or sharecroppers. Sharecropping diminished and with it a primary means by which young families managed to earn a stake that would allow them to buy their own farms, maybe buying out an older farmer they were sharing with.

Sharecroppers in the South, many of them poor blacks, responded in part by forming lobbying organizations like the Southern Tenant Farmers Union to voice their complaints. But it was to little avail. Southern blacks were not well represented in the Congress of 1933, to put it mildly. The Democratic Party was dominant in the southern states, a result of the resentments of Republicans by southern whites dating back to the Civil War. Southern voters were predominantly white, because few blacks were able to overcome the official and unofficial blockage of their access to the ballot box. Complaints from sharecroppers about the policies of the New Deal fell on deaf ears.

To meet its goal of boosting farm prices, the new Agricultural Adjustment Administration not only paid farmers to grow less but also paid them to destroy some of the crops and livestock they had already produced. Some six million baby pigs were slaughtered, a measure that many Americans found repulsive, particularly at a time when there were people in the cities who were not getting enough to eat. Farmers, by and large, treasured their animals. They sometimes even gave them names, in the case of horses and dairy cows. Many people, farmers and townspeople alike, thought it weirdly unnatural to wantonly slaughter and bury pigs and cattle just to lift prices. Southern cotton farmers got $11 an acre to plow under cotton they had already planted, resulting in a reduction of 25 percent of the 1934 cotton crop initially planted.

Prices did rise. In national spot markets a bushel of corn went from an average of 32 cents in 1932 to $1.04 in 1936. Wheat went from 38 cents to $1.02. On March 4, 1933, the Whiteland elevator was paying only 16 cents a bushel for corn and 40 cents for wheat. By October 13, 1936, the prices had gone up to 95 cents for corn and $1.09 for wheat.

The New Dealers hailed this increase as proof that their production quotas had worked. How much of the increase was due to the quotas and how much to the widespread droughts throughout the farm belt in 1934 and 1936 was not discernible, but it's quite likely that the droughts, which created widespread hardship, curbed supply more than government quotas did. The summer of 1936 saw some of the highest average temperatures nationally recorded either before or since. It also isn't clear how many farmers were unable to take advantage of higher prices because their crops had been burnt out. What was clearly visible was that the grocery store prices of bread and corn products went up as their constituent grains rose in cost.

The AAA's subsidies to farmers to reduce production were to be paid for by a tax on food processors, like Stokely and Hougland. That means that not only was the AAA trying to raise prices through market interference, but it also was hitting consumers with a double whammy by passing along the cost of this project with an added cost burden on food companies.

Perhaps the most egregious aspect of the AAA was the amendment authored by populist Oklahoma senator Elmer Thomas. In the simple logic of populism, the senator apparently reasoned that since we were having a revolution, why not go all the way and give our president the power to create money? His amendment gave the president the right to authorize the Federal Reserve to buy up to $3 billion in federal securities, or in other words, inject as much as $3 billion of newly printed money into the economy. Among other trespasses, this violated the Fed's status as an independent agency supposedly free of political pressure. That was always something of a fiction, but that hardly justified the total destruction of the idea that money is too important to be left entirely in the hands of politicians.

This measure anticipated by seventy-five years the Fed's more recent experiment in "quantitative easing," after the 2008 market crash, to try to stimulate the economy by buying trillions in government bonds and mortgage-backed securities. The difference was that Thomas wanted to hand the power to inflate the currency directly to the president, giving a vast power to the chief executive that could be and almost surely would be used politically and sometimes capriciously so. Such power in the hands of a politician was more dangerous than in the hands of the Fed, itself dangerous enough. It was a measure that was more revolutionary at that time than it would seem with regard to the heavily politicized Fed of today

Because of its overextension of executive power and its blatant income transfer from food processors to farmers, the U.S. Supreme Court ruled the AAA unconstitutional in 1935. But Congress rewrote the act. Its system of subsidies, quotas, and market price supports survived the rewrite and in a form altered by successive farm bills, remains on the books in principle even today. This is at a time when most farmers, who now comprise less than 1 percent of the U.S. population, are far from poor. In 2007, according to the USDA, the 585 farms in Johnson County, which average 243 acres each, had an average market value of $1,082,177. On only 263 is farming the principal occupation, but 285 got government support payments.

The diversified cropping of the 1930s is a thing of the

past. Corn and soybeans, planted and harvested with huge $300,000 machines, account for almost all of Indiana's crop production, along with price-supported milk from large dairy herds milked in automated barns. The cabs of the combines are air-conditioned and equipped with modern communications equipment. Many have GPS systems to guide the machines so that the thirty-foot-wide swaths they make going one way are accurately joined together when they come back.

Back in the 1930s, a Fordson tractor pulling a corn planter could cover less than 15 percent of that area at a much slower pace. Expensive modern equipment plus more advanced planting and harvesting methods enable a farmer today to plant and harvest a thousand acres with less toil than his 1930s counterpart put in to handle fifty. His crop yields are much higher, there is very little sweat labor, and he has far more leisure time given efficiency and specialization of the business. And yet he is still subsidized by taxpayers.

★

CHAPTER TWENTY-ONE

THE BLUE EAGLE

IN LATE 1933, dealing with the red tape and constraints of the farm bill was no longer of direct concern to the Melloans. We escaped that when we moved to town. But the AAA wasn't the only New Deal grand-scale experiment. Even more all-encompassing was the National Industrial Recovery Act, whistled through Congress in that same hundred days of revolutionary legislation. The act created the National Recovery Administration (NRA) with a mandate to force prices up through regimentation of American business.

Every American industry would be required to write a "code" setting standards for prices, wages, and other aspects of conducting a business, whether large or small. Since this was to be an exercise in regimentation, putting a general in charge seemed appropriate. FDR put one of his brain trusters, U.S. Army general Hugh Samuel "Iron Pants" Johnson, in charge.

Hugh Johnson was a tough, abrasive man of action and quickly set about his task. The NRA's symbol, a blue eagle, showed up in Whiteland one day in 1933 in the form of a decal posted on the window of the post office. It was an augury of things to come. Thereafter there would be many thousands of blue eagles pasted on windows, accompanied by government propaganda insisting that subscribing to the codes and displaying the blue eagle was an act of patriotism.

In *The Forgotten Man*, Amity Shlaes, a former *Wall Street Journal* editorial board member, writes: "The NRA was the consummation of a thousand articles and a thousand trends. It was the ideas of [Roosevelt brain truster Raymond] Moley, the trade unions, Stuart Chase, Stalin, [utility tycoon Samuel] Insull, Teddy Roosevelt, Henry Ford, and Mussolini's Italian model all rolled into one. The law worked on the assumption that bigger was better and that industry, labor and government must work together, as in Italy, or risk staying in depression. It advocated both greater productivity and greater efficiency while forbidding price cutting, in order to nudge prices up. There was little escaping the NRA. Some 22 million workers came under its 557 basic codes."

The *Greenwood News* was owned by Herbert "Chick" Harris, a large man of a somewhat brooding mien, with a certain weakness for women and booze. He hailed from the southern Indiana resort town called French Lick, where health seekers from the cities went to take the waters. Chick, who would give me my first newspaper job when I came of age, was protective of his editorial independence and fierce in his demands for access to public records, which Greenwood's mayor and town marshal, in the typical style of small-town politicians, sometimes sought to conceal to demonstrate their power and, as often as not, spare themselves embarrassments.

But big, tough Chick was a sucker for the New Deal's propaganda message that it was a patriotic duty of Americans to follow the dictates of Washington and the NRA. He proudly displayed the eagle symbol, in black and white since he couldn't print color, on the front page of his newspaper, thus aiding the federal pressure on businessmen and -women to submit to the heavy-handed effort to herd them into cartels and thereby raise prices to consumers. A great many big business CEOs, such as GE's Swope, loved the NRA because cartels reduced their exposure to competition from more efficient producers or lower-cost start-ups. Their companies had made it big and now they could rest on their laurels, protected by a Democratic president and Congress by federal codes stifling competition.

While the NRA was trying to raise prices, it was urging consumers to buy before prices went up, an egregious bit of government hustling. Chick in 1934 printed an editorial that was straight out of the New Deal propaganda machine, saying, "If we buy now, the new flow in the channels of trade will be increased and accelerated. And that means more production, more men at work, greater circulation of money. . . ." It argued that buying was a patriotic duty and that consumers could actually save money because prices "must go up as part of the reconstruction work of recovery . . . we can win if we buy now."

A line at the bottom of this entreaty said, "[C]ontributed for the purpose of supporting the NRA, by the *Greenwood News*." It never seems to have occurred to Chick that even while he was fighting local political corruption, he was turning over the pages of his newspaper to a flimflam that was national in scope.

The government was trying to raise prices and at the same time squeeze blood out of the hard-pressed citizenry by exhorting them to spend. An explicitly NRA ad in the *Greenwood News* cried out, "Money Spent Makes Work." It exhorted readers: "Let's resolve today to spend more, buy more, consume more!" The NRA propaganda must have sounded a little silly to the schoolteachers and factory workers of Greenwood trying to scrape by on fifteen dollars a week. They would have been happy to buy more, were it not for the troublesome fact that they didn't have the money.

The word from on high had come down to local industries. The Chevrolet Division of General Motors posted an ad in the *News* saying, "We are proud and happy to do our part." Stokely of Greenwood and Noblitt-Sparks, a Greenwood firm making automobile heaters, issued promises to comply with the NRA code. A Greenwood preacher sent a letter to the NRA suggesting a day of prayer for the economy. That probably would have been no less effective than what General Johnson and his underlings were actually attempting with his all-encompassing federal agency.

Charles F. Meier, a Greenwood coal merchant, tried to cash in on the urgings of his national government to buy now before prices went up. He advertised that he was ready to supply coal before the inevitable price increases.

FDR's scheme to cartelize the economy to raise prices would, like the farm act, come a-cropper in the Supreme Court in 1935 when it ruled in the case of *Schecter Poultry Corp. v. United States* that the NRA's efforts to force American industries to adopt "codes of fair competition" were an unconstitutional exercise of federal government power. The court ruling said that the National Industrial Recovery Act (NIRA) delegated too much power to the executive, effectively granting the executive the power to legislate reserved by the Constitution to Congress.

So Chick Harris, rather than exercising the skepticism he applied elsewhere, had willingly signed on to the New Deal's gross abuse of power. He was of course not alone. But even some of the early proponents of the NRA were beginning to lose faith in it by the time the high court quashed it. There was little attempt to revive it, even though FDR was furious at the twin reversals of the NIRA and the AAA. His fury led him to hatch his famous plan to pack the Supreme Court by appointing an additional member for each justice over seventy years and six month of age.

That could have added as many as six FDR appointees to the court, turning it into a body that would bend more easily to the president's wishes, however bizarre the legislation. Even a Democratic Congress wouldn't bite on that and FDR's "Judicial Procedures Reform Bill of 1937" bit the dust.

CHAPTER TWENTY-TWO

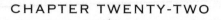

WARNINGS FROM EUROPE

Sis and Sam

T<small>HE DECLINING ENTHUSIASM</small> in the mid-1930s for Washington-concocted statism might have had something to do with what people were seeing in the newspapers and on movie house newsreels at that time. My fellow villagers only had to spend Sunday afternoons at Franklin's Artcraft Theater to watch black-and-white Movietone newsreels depicting state power gone mad in Europe and Asia. They showed the bloody horrors of the attacks on the Chinese by the imperial Japanese army. Germany's Adolf Hitler and Italy's Benito Mussolini could be seen strutting around thrusting their arms skyward and screaming at the tops of their lungs, a tactic that drew great, mindless cheers from huge crowds.

With cross-ocean air traffic in its infancy, in practical terms Europe was a long train ride and a six-day trip by ocean liner away from Indiana. It didn't seem to have much to do with us. So we, at least those of us too young to remember World War I, often regarded these dictators as figures of fun. Perhaps we would have laughed harder if there hadn't been accompanying footage of massive numbers of heavy tanks rolling through the streets of Berlin and Rome and heavy bombers crowding the skies over Europe.

Our elders took them more seriously, a sign of their greater wisdom and experience. Although the threat probably aroused their patriotism, it must also have occurred to them that excessive submission to the police powers of the state could be dangerous to long-cherished liberties. A 1935 satirical novel by Sinclair Lewis titled *It Can't Happen Here* warned of this danger, with its main character very much resembling Huey Long, a demagogic governor of Louisiana with presidential ambitions. In a sign that even New Dealers were waking up to the threat, the WPA produced a stage version of the novel and put it on a nationwide tour. Of course, part of the motivation for the WPA's gambit was to dampen Long's chances to challenge FDR.

FDR would win the election of 1936 in a landslide over Alf

Landon, but he was not able to savor that victory for very long before the stock market crashed again in 1937, touching off what came to be called the "second depression."

In 1934, the American economy was making a recovery from the low point of the Depression in 1932. Unemployment was down from its 1932 level, although it still was very high, at 21.7 percent. There would be gradual improvement into 1936, when the jobless level fell to 16.9 percent of the workforce. That was still very high, but farmers and farm towns were doing better and there were more jobs in the cities.

The Supreme Court's scuttling of the worst excesses of the New Deal in 1935 had helped restore some degree of business confidence. Ambitious people in Whiteland, like the truck drivers mentioned earlier, were still employing their own energies and skills to get ahead in life. Typical of that breed was Sis's husband, Sam Battin.

Sam had a high standing among the town boys. He had played basketball on the same 1929–30 high school team that had also won Babe Baughman popularity. Sam was a regular at the barbershop, where town boys gathered to tell stories, argue issues of the day, and watch Glenn Barnett render haircuts. There wasn't much else to do in off-hours, but loafing at the barbershop was pleasurable enough. In these debates, Sam's contributions were emphatic, often delivered in colorful language and usually tinged with good humor.

Sam also had an important sideline. He was Whiteland's scorekeeper at high school basketball games. Each team had its own scorekeeper to ensure fairness, the lack of which, or even the slightest suspicion thereof, might cause a riot. Sam definitely had the aplomb for this important role. Before a home game, he might stroll to the scorer's bench with clipboard in hand across the shiny, heavily shellacked basketball court, exercising a right to trod on that hallowed hardwood reserved only for players and officials. He wore neatly pressed gray slacks, a gray wool cardigan, and black leather Converse athletic shoes. Casually surveying the crowd, he displayed an attitude of proprietorship, as if the production they were about to witness were his own creation.

His air of savoir faire instilled confidence that the score-keeping would be competent and honest—at least as far as our side was concerned. So everyone could just relax. Of course, if it were a close, hard-fought game, that would hardly be the case. The ambient temperature would be lifted by the heat energy given off by excited fans and the decibel level would become deafening.

The town's sense of identity was tied up in these schoolboy games. Our Warriors were adored by schoolgirls and matrons alike and their drive and agility made middle-aged men recall their own virile youth and shout encouragement. Winning at basketball was important to our mental health.

Sam's family was not part of the Whiteland upper crust, a level attained by only a few, like the Durhams of banking prestige or Charles Graham, a commission agent at the Indianapolis stockyards. But they were relatively well-off by Whiteland standards. They were active in the little Baptist church next door to their house. Old Sam had a steady year-round job as warehouse manager at Stokely's. His eldest daughter, Meredith, was unmarried and a buyer for Wasson's, one of the three frontline department stores in Indianapolis. Old Sam's wife, Nettie, made a little money selling chickens and eggs. Many a time I was assigned to go down to Nettie's to buy a couple of pullets or a dozen eggs. Sam's brother Charlie was married with two daughters and drove a semi for Morgan Packing Company, hauling canned goods hither and yon.

Young Sam was rather handsome, a man of medium build with black wavy hair and a gold tooth that flashed when he grinned, which was often, and often mischievously. Sitting at the kitchen table one day not long after he and Sis married, when they were still living in an apartment at the old Thompson Hotel and Sis was teaching school, Sam said, "If I could just earn thirty-five dollars a week, I'd have it made."

That seemed like an impossible dream in 1934, when even the bosses at Hougland were paying themselves less than thirty dollars a week. Sam was working at Stokely and hoped to eventually succeed his dad as warehouse manager. As warehouse manager, old Sam kept track of the inventory of bottled ketchup, chili sauce, and canned goods stored from the packs. There would be short work stints for other Whitelanders in the off-season loading the cases of food products onto freight cars spotted on the Pennsylvania Railroad siding adjacent to the factory loading platform.

Old Sam had a desirable job because he worked full-time, seeing to it that the incoming orders were filled, manifests written, and shipments properly loaded so they wouldn't be damaged before they got to another warehouse platform somewhere else in the United States. Many Whitelanders were less fortunate, finding work at the factory only during the packs.

Sis and Sam supplemented their income for a while by taking over the Whiteland café and serving up soft drinks, ice cream, and short orders. The restaurant was especially popular during the basketball season as a meeting place after the games. The players, wearing their blue varsity sweaters with a white *W*, would come in after their showers and would often get applause if they won. Walter Martin Umbarger would have his girl and future wife, "Jack" Thompson, Dorothy Jean's sister, on his arm. Norman Shinn, son of Harry and Mildred, would be accompanied by his intended, the pretty Beulah Mae Henry, daughter of Ray and Sadie. It was a cozy, warm setting on winter nights, with the café's front windows steamed up and ballplayers recalling key plays and their maneuvers to fake out their opponents on the other team and get to the basket. We were Whiteland! That was our identity, and the night was especially glorious if we had scored a victory over our archrival, Greenwood.

When old Sam retired in 1937, young Sam desperately wanted to replace him and have the security of a steady, year-round job. The restaurant venture had not been very profitable and the restaurant had passed into the hands of Art and Ruby Palmer, who enjoyed the camaraderie of running a village hangout. When old Sam retired, young Sam was given the job on a temporary basis but factory manager Pat Good decided that it might not be good practice to seem to be establishing a Battin family dynasty. So he gave the permanent job to Bert Good, who, interestingly enough, was not directly related to Pat. Bert had been a loyal warehouse hand and it is my guess that Pat thought he needed the job more than Sam, who was better able than the more elderly Bert to make his way in the world.

If that's what he thought, he was proved to be right. Young Sam was bitterly disappointed, and he and Pat were never on good terms thereafter. But it was all for the best. Like the thousands of other ambitious men who had built the industrial infrastructure of the United States, Sam started his own business.

In the late 1930s, he acquired a used 1936 Ford pickup truck, hired blacksmith Frank Richardson to weld pipe racks on the right side of the truck bed, and, using the knowledge he had picked up assisting Don Parkhurst in maintenance at the canning factory, started doing plumbing. At that stage of American economic history, Sam didn't need a state license or a union membership. Those things would come to Indiana later as tradesmen banded together to get laws that restricted access to their calling, reducing competition and allowing them to charge more. The New Deal had had that same idea for farmers and other businesses when it authored the farm and industrial acts in 1933.

But in Whiteland, the only qualification Sam needed was a reputation for doing good work at a reasonable cost, which he gradually developed. His pipe joints didn't leak. His water pumps, which he wired himself without need of a separate electrician, pumped. His commodes sat straight and tall. There were some complaints about his prices, but then that was normal and the worst mistake a small businessman can make is to undercharge for his services and go broke.

It was a good business. Outdoor privies, of which there were many in Whiteland in the 1930s, were uncomfortable, particularly on a rainy or snowy night. It didn't help much that the WPA was supplying cheap and more modern outhouses, with a fold-up seat, to many homeowners at a reasonable, probably taxpayer-subsidized, cost. They were still outhouses. Indoor plumbing was a high priority for anyone who could scrape a little money together. And usually people who had jobs could do that as the effects of the second depression began to wear off.

Indoor plumbing involved a lot of digging, for the soil pipe leading away from the house, the septic tank, and the filter system. There were no modern machines, like Ditch Witches, for this task. It was done with chalk lines, spades, shovels, and human sweat. Tree roots were severed with saws and rocks extracted with picks.

As his business grew, Sam sometimes hired his nephew Jim Speas and me to dig ditches. He also sometimes used Bart Whitney, a rather dark and moody man who was a good worker, except for the times when he removed himself to Indianapolis to get roaring drunk. Once when we were digging, Bart attempted to explain his drinking problem to me: "I tried to drown my troubles in whiskey, but they learned how to swim."

Touched by this admission of alcoholism, I wondered what difficulties could possibly trouble Bart, a bachelor who lived with his father and bore none of the responsibilities of a man with a wife and family. But of course his difficulties were within himself, the psychic pain that demands relief and that can be eased temporarily with large doses of alcohol. Bart's trouble was likely an affliction of the body, not necessarily of the soul.

Even manual labor, if done well, commanded respect in 1930s Whiteland. The best ditchdigger in town, or maybe even the county, was Walter Thomas, a compact, muscular man of about fifty usually seen in tan canvas trousers tucked into knee-high black rubber boots, the costume of his trade. Walter had advanced ditchdigging to an art form. His ditches were straight and true. They had just the right amount of slope from the house to the septic tank, and the hole for that large, tile cylinder was dug to the proper depth, so that when it was heaved into the hole, its opening exactly matched the level of the soil pipe ditch from the house. Walter could charge Sam more than the rest of us could ask, 70 cents an hour versus our 50. But he was faster, more accurate, and hence worth the extra pay.

From his modest beginning, Sam built a sizable business. He was turned down for military service by the draft board in 1940 because of an eczema condition, so he was able to build up capital by working at an Indianapolis defense plant, Bridgeport Brass, making artillery shells during the war. Starting up again in the late 1940s, he could again get pipes, fittings, and fixtures. In the 1950s, he expanded to a business with five employees, four trucks, and the ability to take on big jobs, like the plumbing and heating for the new Johnson County hospital. He would fulfill his dream of making thirty-five dollars a week, and then some.

CHAPTER TWENTY-THREE

★

A STORE ON THE "CAR LINE"

IN 1936, MOM also went into business, renting the grocery store across from the Linco station on the "car line." Our store was also the Interurban station and we sold tickets. A bench on the front porch of our store was the waiting area, although commuters stood inside on cold or rainy days. During winter ice storms, the Interurbans put on a spectacular fireworks display, as they crept along with their trolleys skipping over the ice and shooting off sparks. It was especially impressive at night. Mom and I rode the Interurban to Franklin every Saturday to visit the library, where I searched for boys' adventure books and Mom picked up her week's supply of mystery novels.

It was fun for Marie and me to hang around the store, wait on customers (although we were not allowed to use the lunch meat slicer), and occasionally nibble on some of the wares. Clara Evelyn Heck, a slender, fun-loving tomboy whose family lived across the street from our house in Old Whiteland, was visiting Marie at the store one day when a young salesman came in to introduce us to a new product, RC Cola. He gave us each paper cups for sampling this wonder drink. Clara Evelyn downed a cup, said she couldn't make up her mind, and asked for more. Marie and I caught on to this game and did the same. We weren't fooling the salesman, but he seemed to enjoy our teasing as much as we did. And we finally gave his cola our approval, although we were not authorized to buy any for the store's chipped-ice soft drink cooler.

Clara Evelyn's father, Todd, worked as a machinist in Indianapolis and remained employed throughout the Depression. The six Hecks took vacations in the summer—something unknown to families like ours—going to "the lakes" somewhere in northern Indiana for fishing and swimming.

Todd was a tubby German with a gravelly voice and somewhat forbidding in appearance. But every Fourth of July, he supplied the neighborhood kids with a rare form of entertainment. Poking out of a port in the balustrade of the

Hecks' brick front porch was a small cannon. On the morning of every Fourth, every year at precisely eleven o'clock, Todd would load the cannon with a blank shotgun shell and fire it. It spit fire and made a great boom. With the ceremony complete, Todd would go back into the house to utilize the rest of the holiday by enjoying his wife's good cooking, listening to the Cubs game on the radio, and having a few bottles of Schlitz.

There seemed to be a message in this ceremony. Maybe Todd's cannon reflected a fortress mentality derived from the ancestrial keeper of some ancient *schloss*. Or maybe beneath that gruff exterior was a man who, like his daughter Clara Evelyn, just wanted to have fun.

But back to the car line. Once a caravan of three big cars packed with gypsies, with their luggage piled high on top, came up Highway 31 and parked across from our store. The rule followed by most merchants was to lock the door to gypsies, but we weren't fast enough and they came crowding into the store. They paid for some things and palmed others. Where they came from and where they were heading, no one ever seemed to know, but they seemed prosperous, judging from their cars and jewelry. To this day, I remain puzzled over the question of what ever happened to the gypsies of America.

The store adventure lasted only a year or so. Mom was both a storekeeper and part-time counselor to those among her customers who were troubled by fear or doubt. Presumably it was because they instinctively knew she was a good listener and might have good advice. One spring day, the proprietor of another store plunked himself down on a stool at our small food counter and started crying. He told Mom that his wife had run off with another man, a farmer who also was married with children. The wife in question, a quiet, rather plain woman, seemed an unlikely candidate for a marital escapade, but who knows what secret romantic thoughts or sexual fantasies she had been harboring as she played the spouse of a respectable businessman?

Mom told the grieving man that his wife probably would come back and beg his forgiveness. She did, after a week's holiday in Chicago with her paramour. The farmer returned to his wife as well, and I would like to say they all lived happily ever after, but in fact I have no idea.

Sara Ollie

Mom's empathy, which drew people to her for advice, was not necessarily a business asset. She couldn't resist extending credit to the poor migrant workers from the Kentucky hills who came up to work in the tomato pack, some to pick tomatoes in the fields and others to work at the Stokely plant. Some camped out in tents near the fields. Others found shelter in barns or cleaned-up former henhouses available for cheap rent.

Mom was herself a Kentuckian and had known her share of hardship. These were her people and, even though we weren't well off ourselves, she could identify with their struggles to keep body and soul together. Some eventually settled their accounts when they began to earn money, but others never did, or never could. The losses depleted our cash balance and we finally gave up and moved back to the big house in Old Whiteland that had been rented out to the Robards family during our sojourn at the car line.

At about that time, Dad decided to have one more try at farming. He rented twenty acres of land along Grassy Creek from Uncle Bert, and we put in tomatoes. Marie and I dropped the plants and Bob and Jim did the setting. But again it all ended in sorrow. I well remember the sad day some weeks later, after heavy rains, when George Money, the Stokely field agent, came by to tell us that Grassy Creek had overflowed its banks and washed out our crop. It was Dad's last big defeat.

CHAPTER TWENTY-FOUR

★

THE SECOND CRASH

Dᴜʀɪɴɢ ᴛʜᴇ 1936 general election, FDR kept pounding away at his favorite bogeyman, Wall Street, in his campaign against the Republican nominee, Alf Landon. His campaign slogan was "Landon and Wall Street, Roosevelt and Main Street. Which do you prefer?" (Does that sound familiar in the age of Bernie Sanders and Hillary Clinton?) He won decisively partly because

of his celebrated oratorical skills, the weak but nonetheless reassuring economic recovery, and his ability over the preceding
four years, with the able help of his postmaster general, James
A. Farley, to build a powerful national political machine.

Farley had masterminded FDR's New York gubernatorial
campaigns and his initial 1932 presidential victory. He is
credited with having the insight to recognize the electoral
potential of the newly formed Congress of Industrial Organizations (CIO), a factory union federation more militant than
the old AFL. The CIO had gained many adherents because of
the Depression hardships of industrial workers.

FDR's antibusiness speechifying was partly designed to
win the CIO's loyalty and it succeeded. FDR's critics have
alleged that he and Farley also were not above favoring Democratic Party loyalists in handing out federally financed WPA
jobs. If that was true, it certainly wasn't the first or last time
political patronage figured in American elections. The rarer
instances have been when it didn't.

The president was also helped by the improving economy.
Unemployment had dropped from its high of almost a quarter of the labor force in 1933 to just under 17 percent in 1936.
That was still very high but the decline allowed the Democrats
to claim that their revolutionary measures had brought about
economic improvement. Claims like that are often persuasive
in politics, partly because it is difficult to differentiate the effects of policy from the effects of other economic forces.

At any rate, the country was feeling a bit better in 1936.
In Indiana, Democrat Clifford Townsend won the governorship, succeeding Paul V. McNutt, the handsome, silver-haired

Democrat who was no slouch himself in machine building. FDR, in a fit of pique at McNutt's obtuseness at the 1932 Democratic convention, once called him "that bleached blond s.o.b. from Indiana."

But high finance would again come unglued in 1937, when the Fed once again raised interest rates and the markets crashed, taking with them, as in 1929, the jobs market as well. After having been as low as 14.3 percent in 1937, the average rate of unemployment soared back up to 19 percent in 1938. It would remain high until World War II. Hougland Packing in Franklin would again suffer a loss in 1938, after prospering in the mid-1930s.

The causes of this sudden reverse have been widely debated, but conservatives have attributed it not only to a loss of business confidence resulting from the antibusiness rhetoric of the Democrats' campaign but also to legislation in what was called the "second New Deal." For one thing, the Democrats had passed an "undistributed profits" tax on income surpluses reported by corporations in their annual reports. The New Deal's idea behind this unprecedented measure was that it would not only raise revenue but force corporations to distribute more of their profits to shareholders and employees.

Even some ranking Treasury employees in FDR's administration advised against this tax, calling it a dumb idea. It seems not to have occurred to the Democrats who passed it or FDR, who signed it, that corporations use their undistributed profits to plow money back into the business and grow new jobs. Taxing that money away was in truth a means of taxing away jobs. FDR finally seems to have caught on, after the reverses of 1937 and 1938, and the tax was eliminated in 1939.

The second New Deal included some new brainstorms from Rexford Tugwell, including a plan to resettle millions of Americans to government communities, but Tugwell was wearing thin even with Democrats by then. His plan got little traction in Congress and in 1941 Roosevelt dispatched him to the governorship of Puerto Rico, getting him out of the way of the war effort. A recent governor of the island told a friend of mine that Puerto Rico is still living with the damage caused by Tugwell's schemes to reorder the local economy.

Another blow to business confidence was the National Labor Relations Act of 1935, known as the Wagner Act, which gave unions stronger rights to organize workers, engage in collective bargaining, and enforce their demands with strikes. A wave of strikes ensued as CIO unions organized employees in two of the nation's largest industries, autos and steel. The NLRA was a boon to labor unions but it didn't do much for economic efficiency. Real wages rose 11.6 percent in 1937 without a corresponding increase in productivity.

Also in early 1937, employers and employees were burdened with the advent of payroll taxes legislated to finance the new Social Security law, which initially took more out of the economy than it put back in. In mid-1937, the economy was hit by a sharp downturn. Over the next thirteen months, industrial production fell by 30 percent. The stock market crash was more gradual but deeper than the one eight years earlier. The Dow Jones Industrials fell by almost 50 percent between early 1937 and March 1938. By comparison, the decline from September 1929 to May 1930 was 25 percent.

Some theorists think monetary policy was mainly to blame

and there's some plausibility to that argument. Roosevelt's reflationary policy of 1933 was a success, but only partly because of the measures he and the Fed took, including raising the price of gold, to inflate the money supply. Between 1933 and 1936, the money stock expanded by 46 percent and prices rose 31 percent. This, however, was due mainly to an inflow of gold from Europe, as the totalitarian aims of Hitler and Mussolini raised more and more disquiet in financial circles.

Concerned about the dangers of inflation, the U.S. Treasury and the Fed in 1936 decided to apply monetary countermeasures, withdrawing money from circulation, to "sterilize" the gold inflows. This certainly crimped credit, but whether it was the primary cause of the crash, as monetarists Milton Friedman and Anna Schwartz averred, is still debated. It seems quite likely that both the monetary measures and the new laws of the second New Deal were to blame. Large perturbations are usually caused by a combination of factors.

The Wagner Act of 1935 had given unions stronger bargaining powers while at the same time putting management on the defensive. The CIO and member unions like the United Auto Workers (UAW) and United Steelworkers became militant and owners and managers resisted their demands. That, coupled with hard times and the corporation-baiting by FDR in his fireside chats, created labor tensions that generated frequent strikes, some of which turned violent, as when Ford Motor Company security forces tangled with UAW organizers in the 1937 Battle of the Overpass at Ford's River Rouge plant in Detroit. One organizer suffered a broken back.

Although FDR had no way of knowing it at the time, the labor militancy he encouraged would ultimately bring results contrasting with the economic damage it did in the 1930s. An argument could be made that union contracts priced labor costs at higher than market rates and ultimately opened the door to the establishment of nonunion plants in the United States by foreign auto and steel companies. Labor strife also encouraged American managers to forge better relationships with their employees. Corporations sprouted "human relations" departments. Over time, industrial workers saw less need to join unions and pay them dues. Union membership rose sharply in the late 1930s to almost 20 percent of the non-farm workforce in 1939 and continued to almost a third of that workforce by 1953. But since the late 1970s it has been in steady decline and today only about 11 percent of members of the workforce carry a union card; public employee unions account for about 60 percent of that small share.

Roosevelt was something of a political genius but there always were doubts about his grasp of the issues his administration was confronting and whether he bothered to examine crucial details of the legislation his followers were drafting. Barney Kilgore, a *Wall Street Journal* Washington bureau chief and columnist in the 1930s and later the CEO of Dow Jones, attended a press session in the Oval Office in 1936 in which the new Social Security law came up for discussion.

In those days, presidential press conferences often were informal gatherings in the Oval Office of reporters from the wire services and important newspapers. They were nothing like the big productions of today, with TV lights blazing and an auditorium full of journalists, each vying for the limelight. One of the group gathered around FDR's desk in 1936 asked him a question about a rather recondite part of this new law that would become so important to Americans. FDR smiled and said, "I'll bet Barney Kilgore can answer that for you."

Barney could indeed answer the question because he had read the new law from top to bottom. He later told friends that he believed FDR fobbed off the question on him because FDR didn't know the answer himself. The cagey president knew Barney, a bright man, would likely know the answer. But he also knew that it would be embarrassing to Barney, after the president's buildup, if he didn't know it. FDR might have enjoyed inflicting some embarrassment on a frequent critic of his New Deal experiments. Barney's column had once warned American corporations against cutting the NRA cartel deal with FDR, warning them that in any partnership with the government, Uncle Sam would always be the senior partner. They had to learn that the hard way. It's a lesson that corporate leaders seem to have to learn repeatedly, as evidenced by the buyer's remorse that some companies, like Netflix, are feeling after backing the Obama government's recent "net neutrality" takeover of the Internet. The competitive edge they thought they were getting came with a lot of regulatory strings attached, just as onetime corporate backers of the blue eagle learned in the 1930s.

Although the Depression came roaring back in 1937, the Whiteland economy had been on the mend for the preceding four years. An article in the *Franklin Evening Star* in 1935 reported a robust tomato pack at the Whiteland Stokely plant.

The *Star* wrote that the factory employed about 550 workers with a payroll averaging $85,000 to $90,000.

That meant that the average worker made $154 to $164. Of course, Pat Good and other managers made more than the average and hourly workers less. But if a married couple could earn $200 in the pack, that money could keep them going for quite some time at 1935 price levels. The factory contracted for 1,100 to 1,200 acres of tomatoes that year, giving local farmers a boost as well.

Indiana was the country's third-ranking producer of tomatoes in 1935, behind Maryland and California. Factories in the state packed 3,587,000 cases of tomatoes that year, each containing twenty-four number-two cans. Today that industry has virtually disappeared, as tomato packing has been subsumed by big highly automated agribusinesses in places like California and Florida.

Despite the omens of a new slump, the pack was again a happy time for people of the village. The aroma of cooking ketchup and chili sauce wafted through the town. Trucks and wagons stacked high with hampers of the red fruit lined up on the county road, waiting to be weighed and unloaded at the Stokely dock.

As always, there were a few sour notes. Canning companies reserved the right to "dock" farmers if the factory inspector judged their tomatoes to be of poor quality. That kind of decision, costly to the farmer, often caused resentment. Canners later happily turned over the chore to federal inspectors to relieve themselves of the complaints and bestow them on the feds.

Because of the time needed to pick the tomatoes, the loads

often came in late in the day. This meant that some drivers often were on line late at night, drowsing on a roadside blanket or in the cabs of their trucks. During the pack, the factory ran until midnight trying to process the day's offering. Workers at the factory would often put in fifteen-hour shifts to keep the processing going.

After the outset of World War II took millions of adult males out of the workforce, canning factories had to rely on teenagers, women, or men beyond draft age. After I became eligible for a work permit at age sixteen my first job was cooking chili sauce. My partner and I were in charge of three huge copper vats with copper steam coils at the bottom of each. We would open spigots to pour in a measured amount of tomato pulp, turn on the steam to bring it to a boil, then dump in spices mixed according to a proprietary formula by the factory chemist, two buckets of peeled onions, and ten buckets of peeled tomatoes brought up by elevator from the peeling line staffed by local women on the platform down below.

To avoid burns, we developed a special technique for dumping the buckets, holding the bottom so that our hands were never directly over the scalding steam coming up from the vat. It was also wise to wear a long-sleeved shirt because the hot liquid would sometimes splash out of the vat. Better to have it hit your shirt than bare skin.

Even though our compartment was vented by banks of windows above the vats, on humid days the compartment would get foggy with steam and the wooden platform from which we dumped our buckets would become slippery. The onion peeling machine was an archaic affair with exposed wiring carrying 220 voltage, so it was best to treat it very carefully.

An inspector from today's Occupational Health and Safety Administration would have had apoplexy at our working conditions, but there were no OSHA inspectors then. We were young and free-spirited, so we endured and even, in some perverse way, enjoyed the dangers. Someone started a tomato fight one day, but it ceased quickly when the grim visage of Pat Good suddenly emerged from the stairway opening that led to our floor. Lucky for us, there was a labor shortage.

The worst part of the job was cleaning the coils after the day's runs. You hosed them down with cold water but they still had heat in them when you climbed in to scrub them down with steel wool, often near midnight after a long day of chili sauce cooking. After that arduous task, I would climb out, trudge home, shed my sauce-splattered clothing, and fall into bed exhausted, only to get up the next morning for the same routine. But I was making money, sometimes seven dollars a day, which meant I was making more in a week than some schoolteachers were making, unless the teacher also happened to be working in the pack. Making good money when money is scarce can be an exhilarating experience.

An acre of tomatoes would fetch a farmer somewhere from $40 to $50, out of which he had to pay for planting, cultivating, and harvesting. The factory supplied the tomato plants and hampers. A farmer planting 40 acres could gross around $1,800, with costs running perhaps half that amount.

So tomatoes were a good cash crop for that era. But as with so many things connected with farming, there was never any certainty that things would work out as planned. Maybe a crop would be washed out by heavy rain, or be stunted by tomato blight or destroyed by drought.

Later, I graduated to an easier job, running what for no discernible reason was called a "submarine." This was the machine at platform level that pulped tomatoes and pumped the thick liquid to the cooking vats upstairs. Mostly I just sat on a stool and read a book as the machine went through its twenty-minute cycles. One day when I was so absorbed, someone shouted, "The factory is on fire!" I assumed this was just another of the many games we teenage, wartime factory hands were fond of playing, so at first I took no notice. But Stokely's really was on fire, reportedly because of an overheated warehouse elevator motor.

We tried fighting it with factory hoses. Pat Good inexplicably ordered us to open doors and windows, which may have reduced the risk of smoke inhalation but seemed to fan the flames. The little Whiteland fire truck was useless. We finally retired to a neighboring field and watched the factory burn to the ground, destroying the town's main source of employment and the most convenient marketplace for local farmers. This was in 1944.

It was a tragedy for the older folks. But with 12 million Americans having been mobilized for war, there were plenty of good-paying jobs for the able-bodied and sentient. Sam Battin had suspended his plumbing practice and gone to

Bridgeport Brass Corporation in Indianapolis to help make artillery shell casings. Sis had taken a summer job at the Allison division of General Motors in the city, inspecting ball bearings for aircraft engines. Marie also worked on the engine line. Bill, who also had been rejected for service because of an arm injury he had suffered in an auto accident in 1934, was running the Stokely plant in Tampa, Florida. Connie, rejected because of hernias, was a government food inspector in Plant City, Florida. Meb was a bookkeeper for Pure Oil Company in Indianapolis. I would move to Stokely Van Camp in Indianapolis, slicing pork for pork and beans. I became a member of the UAW at Van Camp. Bob and Jim were in the service.

★

CHAPTER TWENTY-FIVE

OTHER WAR STORIES

ON MONDAY MORNING, December 8, 1941, the day after the Japanese attack on Pearl Harbor, readers of the *Wall Street Journal* saw something they had never seen before: a banner three-tiered headline announcing that we were at war, a condition that would be formalized that day by President Roosevelt's "Day of Infamy" speech denouncing the attack and by a congressional declaration of war. The *Journal*'s lead story, written by managing editor William Kerby under the pressure of a late-afternoon deadline, began with the sentence, "War with Japan means an industrial revolution in the United States." Indeed it did, as the nation's shareholder-owned private corporations plunged into a remarkable feat of industrial mobilization.

A page-one editorial by editor William H. Grimes said that the attack had changed everything in the public debate (meaning that the partisan strife that had roiled American politics in the 1930s must end) and everyone's duty to win the war "will be performed." The *Journal*, a critic of the New Deal, thus lined up behind FDR's wartime leadership.

Fourteen-year-old Jo Minner, my future wife, was jitter-bugging with her younger brother Richard in the living room of their Franklin house on the fateful Sunday afternoon when the music on the radio stopped for a special bulletin: "Japanese planes have just attacked the American naval base at Pearl Harbor in Hawaii."

They ran to tell their mother, Mary, who was working in the kitchen. She burst into tears. She knew her eldest son, Bob, then seventeen, would probably have to fight, as had her husband, Harry, in World War I. Harry had been in the battle of Château-Thierry in France before being hospitalized with diphtheria. A disease that had cost many lives in those days may have saved his.

She was right. In one of his more stupid moves, Hitler would declare war on the United States shortly after the Pearl Harbor attack, thus inviting a powerful newcomer to his array of foes. Bob was drafted after he turned eighteen and was assigned to a combat engineer battalion that was dispatched to Europe. Like his father, he would fight in France. Years later he would tell his sister that his platoon was once pinned down by German fire in a Normandy apple orchard. Only he and his first sergeant were still alive when reinforcements arrived. He would help build a pontoon bridge across the Rhine under fire to enable the Allied armies to penetrate the German homeland. At war's end, his unit ended its long campaign in Austria.

My brother Jim had already joined the army, despite a bad right eye injured in a firecracker accident two years earlier. At Camp Custer in Wyoming, he had disguised his disability by sighting his ancient Springfield rifle, a holdover from World War I, with his left eye. That entailed reaching over with his right hand to operate the primitive bolt action. He became part of an army air-sea rescue team and learned "hard-hat" diving, that is, wearing an old-fashioned diving suit with a global steel helmet connected to a surface boat by an air hose. He served in the Pacific searching for downed pilots. Once on a Pacific island where his team had landed looking for a lost plane, the natives had flowers in their hair, signifying there had been a death. He and his team put flowers in their hair and were led to the crashed airplane and its dead pilot.

Dave Espin, an orphan who had lived with us under the county's foster care program, which had brought many homeless youths under Mom's wing throughout the 1930s, also was of military age. Dave, a husky lad with a face somewhat like the Alfred E. Neuman of *Mad* magazine fame, was a jolly presence. He would sometimes walk home from school singing loudly in his excellent baritone such lyrics as "Give me some men who are stout-hearted men," from the operetta *New*

Moon. Before Dave left for the army, he dropped in at lunchtime to say goodbye. "They may get me, but I'll take some of them with me!" he declared.

I thought that sounded a bit theatrical but my mind was shutting out the reality that the whole point of war was to engage young men in mortal combat as quickly as possible. Dave would soon be thrust into battle in the Pacific. He had a rough war and a difficult postwar psychological recovery. But he made a comeback and became a successful school administrator.

Brother Bob, doing maintenance work at the International Harvester plant in Indianapolis in 1941, listened to Roosevelt's Monday speech with our family. He would soon join the Army Air Corps, serving in North Africa and Italy as a crew chief on fighter planes. His unit moved northward with the Allied campaign in Italy, ending the war at a base near Foggia where P-47s were being launched on bombing and strafing missions against the German forces. The P-47 was popular with pilots on strafing missions because its big radial engine up front and its armored bucket seat offered some protection from ground fire. As with many veterans, Bob never said much about his experiences, in particular how many planes he had sent out that never came back.

He did tell of one happy coincidence. On landing in Italy, Bob's troopship docked alongside another troopship in Naples harbor. Bob spotted on the deck of the other ship his friend Pete Duncan from Whiteland. They yelled to each other, exchanging hometown news. But their units disembarked, going their separate ways, and they never saw each other again until after the war. One of Bob's friends, a farm boy sailor named Warren Shriver, was lost in the Pacific when his ship was sunk by Japanese aircraft. That Whiteland suffered only one loss from such a massive conflict was not bad, but then Whiteland was not a very big town.

President Roosevelt's radio address after Pearl Harbor would inaugurate the wartime leadership that would rescue his reputation from the failures of New Deal programs, such as the ill-conceived NRA. In 1936, he had won labor backing by sometimes launching vicious attacks on "big business." He had won a third term in 1940 because voters wanted an experienced leader if America should become embroiled in war. For that very same reason, FDR knew he would desperately need the mass production skills of the big corporations he had once excoriated, to fashion the weapons of war. His tone toward big business became markedly conciliatory.

Corporations responded magnificently. Ford Motor Company built the huge Willow Run aircraft plant thirty miles west of Detroit in nine months, less time than it would take to get a permit from the Environmental Protection Agency today. Workers at Willow Run were soon building Liberator bombers on a three-quarter-mile assembly line. At its wartime peak in 1944, Willow Run was turning out one bomber an hour, a theretofore unheard-of rate for producing large aircraft, or for that matter, any kind of aircraft. Liberators, eight thousand of which were built at Willow Run, were a key weapon in bringing Germany to its knees.

On the West Coast, Henry Kaiser used methods learned from Ford to quickly convert his shipbuilding yards to

mass-producing "Liberty" ships to transport arms and supplies to the war fronts. On average, they launched a ship
every forty-five days and in November 1942 actually built the
10,500-ton SS *Robert Peary* in a little less than five hours, a feat
equivalent to Ford's Willow Run achievements. Many other big
companies—General Electric, General Motors, Douglas, U.S.
Steel, Alcoa, etc.—executed similar transformations.

The managerial and organizational skills that had enabled
these miracles had been learned in the competitive economy
of the 1930s, when corporations had struggled to rapidly improve the quality of their products in order to winkle scarce
dollars out of consumers. Privately owned American companies quickly became the "Arsenal of Democracy," unmatched
by any productive system in the history of the world.

A few days after D-Day, in June 1944, I was in a field south
of Whiteland dropping tomato plants for German and Italian
war prisoners to set. They were from Camp Atterbury south
of Franklin and under the Geneva Conventions could be employed so long as they were compensated. My prisoners that
day were a tough bunch of German Afrika Korps boys who had
been captured during the successful U.S. and British campaign
to expel General Erwin Rommel's army from North Africa.

When we were out of earshot of the young American
guard, a German who spoke English asked me how far the
Allies had advanced in Normandy. I had seen a headline that
morning and I replied 108 miles. When he translated this to
his fellow soldiers, they became agitated and gathered around
me, shouting. If that were true, it would have meant the Allies
were two-thirds of the way to Paris. Actually, it wasn't true.

The Allies had established a *perimeter* of 108 miles. I had not deliberately misled them. I had simply misread the headline.

The guard came running to see what was going on and ordered us all back to work. The shock of my report to the German prisoners was understandable. They obviously knew that the Allies had succeeded in establishing a beachhead in France, the most important hurdle in bringing the war back to the German homeland, where their families lived. It was dawning on them that despite Hitler's boasts they might now lose the war.

They were of course right. When they could finally go home it would be to a place they would hardly know, a devastated homeland where every one of them would find that he had lost friends and family members to the adventure their leader had begun in 1938 with an attack on Czechoslovakia. With so much housing destroyed, even finding shelter would be a problem. Still, they were lucky. Having been captured in Africa, they were still alive.

I sat beside one man on the bus going back to camp who probably would not be so lucky. He told me in English that he was not German, but one of the Ukrainians who had joined up with the Germans out of hatred for the atrocities that Stalin had committed in Ukraine. I have no way of knowing, but he might have been a victim of the atrocious Operation Keelhaul, in which the Western Allies returned Soviet citizens who had fought for the Germans to their homeland after the war and to a certain death at the hands of a vengeful Stalin.

CHAPTER TWENTY-SIX

WAR'S AFTERMATH

After the war, when I had turned draft age, I would serve an eighteen-month stint in the army, just enough to earn me sufficient GI Bill aid to get a bachelor of science degree in journalism at Butler University in Indianapolis. The army was being rapidly demobilized in 1946 and 1947 and was in a state of confusion. Some captains and majors who had led troops in battle had chosen to be busted back to their former noncom ranks in order to stay in the army and ultimately draw a pension. Newly commissioned eighteen-year-old second lieutenants outranked these veteran first sergeants and master sergeants, but battle-hardened former officers found it difficult to accept the leadership of young "shavetails."

At Fort Knox, where I was myself an eighteen-year-old getting basic training in the art of driving tanks and operating their weapons, I was once called before a small group of senior officers to give them my advice on this matter. I assume they chose me because I had had two trimesters at Purdue. It was a heady experience for a private to be asked to give advice to majors and captains. I told them that if I were a young lieutenant in charge of a contemptuous veteran I would have a quiet chat with him and explain that I understood his feelings but the rules say I outranked him. If that didn't work, I would attempt to find him another assignment. The officers thanked me politely for this pithy advice, which no doubt offered nothing they hadn't thought of themselves.

Some of the soldiers I met were combat veterans. Once I was walking to the Post Exchange at Fort Campbell, Kentucky, for an evening beer with a pleasant young corporal in my unit. He had seen house-to-house fighting in Germany. Once, he said, he had stormed into a darkened room and, hearing a noise behind, he turned and fired his carbine. Only then did he realize he had killed an elderly German couple who were trying to give themselves up. A sensitive lad, he would live with that memory forever.

A tough-looking staff sergeant in my barracks, who because of his rank rated a private room, could be heard screaming at night as he suffered through nightmares reliving his wartime experiences. War is indeed hell.

Wars are only good for the economy if you win, and even that is subject to some doubt. It was easy to see the contrast between the winner of World War II, the United States with its basic infrastructure untouched by bombs or shells, and the losers, war-devastated Germany and Japan, the latter with two of its large cities obliterated by atom bombs. But even some of the "winners," England, France, and the Soviet Union, among others, suffered heavy economic damage.

The United States emerged from the war as the engineer and financier of reconstruction. Remarkably, that undertaking fared best in Japan and Germany, the two main losers. Perhaps that was because they embraced many of the American economic principles that had been revived through the necessities of rapid mobilization. Harry Truman, who had succeeded FDR after his death in office in 1945, was a New Dealer but had a more practical turn of mind than some of the erstwhile revolutionaries. Americans had gained a renewed respect for capitalism and the ability of private corporations to adapt quickly to the vast changes needed to tool up for war and then do it all over again to supply pent-up demand for cars, houses, and appliances after the end of the war.

We were a market capitalist country again after the experiments in government economic management of the New Deal era. Vestiges of those experiments would remain even to this day, but would no longer threaten to convert the U.S.

economic and social system into something radically different from what had brought such a huge improvement in living standards and the quality of life in the nation's first 150 years. Postwar governments led by both Republicans and Democrats promoted free international trade and more rational tax and spending policies.

Among most of our European allies, by contrast, socialism was the order of the day. The Soviet Union's centrally planned command economy had mobilized sufficiently to hold up its end of the war, but the cumbersome system in the 1950s, as before the war, was totally inadequate to the task of filling the needs of a war-battered civilian population. Moreover, Stalin was using his military power and secret police to spread his failed policies throughout the central European countries. Poland, Czechoslovakia, Hungary, and Bulgaria, and to some degree Romania and Yugoslavia, had come within his ambit when the Nazi empire collapsed, and thus they suffered the same retardation of recovery that afflicted their Soviet masters.

British voters had voted in Labourite Clement Attlee as the war ended. The Labour Party's goal was to socialize the British economy, which it set about doing by nationalizing basic industries like steel and autos. As a consequence, Britain lagged far behind Japan and Germany, which had suffered far more damage but had adopted policies more similar to those of America, in recovering from the war.

Newly liberated France had a strong socialist bloc, and even a sizable Communist Party that had distinguished itself in fighting a guerrilla war against the Nazis. War hero Charles de Gaulle, who emerged as France's leader after liberation, succeeded in preventing a Communist Party takeover, but it was a close-run thing and he was in no position to install the type of free market capitalism that was enjoying a comeback in the United States, even if he had wanted to.

European workers, their political consciousness raised by the exigencies of war, wanted better working conditions and better living standards than they had had before the war. By opting for moribund state ownership of the "means of production" and swallowing the Kool-Aid of the socialists, they picked the wrong way to get them.

From being the world's arsenal during the war, the United States became the world's banker. The U.S. dollar, linked to gold at $35 an ounce for central bank exchange purposes, was the keystone of the new Bretton Woods international monetary system, which was designed to facilitate trade and investment by stabilizing the rates at which national currencies could be exchanged.

American private corporations were soon back to supplying America's pent-up demand for consumer goods and expanding abroad to fill similar needs. Europe, with American encouragement, was beginning to shape new institutions, such as the Common Market, with the hope of never again becoming the bloody battleground it had been for centuries. Europe gradually and painfully outlived the worst of socialist ravages, particularly after the Soviet Union collapsed in 1991. It has learned from America. The main question today is whether America learned anything from the postwar European socialist experience.

CHAPTER TWENTY-SEVEN

★

THE GREATEST GENERATION?

FORMER NBC COMMENTATOR Tom Brokaw wrote a book some years ago calling the Americans who came of age during the Depression and fought in World War II the "Greatest Generation." It is a mark of Brokaw's perceptiveness that he chose to honor a people rather than their government. The American people responded with gratitude for that acknowledgment by buying lots of his books.

I didn't make the cut because I was too young to have any real responsibilities in either the Depression or the war. It would be nice to think of my older siblings as historical heroes, and certainly we all had a deep affection for each other. But in truth they were ordinary people doing what they could do to make a living during the Depression and serving their country when that became paramount.

They were only human, and indeed also only human were the people we chose to govern us through the 1920s and '30s. As I have detailed here, whether they called themselves Republicans or Democrats, they made some very big mistakes, often because of unjustified confidence in their abilities to command and control complex forces and sometimes merely out of a desire to satisfy important voting constituencies.

When those attitudes ran counter to the basic principles that normally guide human transactions—for example a mutual agreement on price and terms between a buyer and seller of goods, services, or labor—they often came a cropper. Price fixing by a central authority is a sure formula for economic stagnation or worse, as hundreds of experiments by governments, including our own, have demonstrated over the years.

The old Soviet Union, even by using harsh police state methods, could never pull the people it governed out of poverty. It was a massive experiment in price fixing. That's why it collapsed and why a similar effort by Mao Zedong descended into a nightmare for the Chinese people. Deng Xiaoping, Mao's successor, wisely embraced a form of market capitalism in 1979, with spectacular success in terms of economic growth and a rising standard of living for many millions of Chinese.

Both Herbert Hoover and Franklin D. Roosevelt tried to fight the normal business cycles that result from the ever-changing levels and sources of supply and demand, cycles that require price adjustments to keep the two in balance. Hoover disturbed these adjustments by bringing corporate CEOs into his embrace and asking them to resist wage and price cuts. Roosevelt disturbed them by vilifying business corporations and their bankers and trying to regiment them into an incredibly complex and unworkable regime of artificial pricing of both goods and labor, better known as the NRA.

The people of my village were like those everywhere, in that there were among us people of intelligence and some not so bright, paragons of honesty and some a little shady, upholders of virtue and some less observant of prevailing community standards. But on one vital score they were different from the villagers of Europe, Asia, Africa, or Latin America at that time. Their cultural and political heritage had bequeathed to them more control over their lives and fates than most peoples elsewhere in the world.

In short, their freedoms and individuality had better legal protections, under the American Constitution and legal precedents, than most people then, and maybe even Americans now. That often-used word *freedom* might sound like a cliché to many modern ears and there are even some Americans who too often utter "there oughta be a law" that would further curb those freedoms.

But people I have met who have suffered under political tyranny, even the soft tyranny of what still remains of the British class system, understand clearly that American "exceptionalism" is a synonym for "freedom." They understand the difference that word makes in the quality of one's life.

The people of America and of most parts of the world are far better off today than they were eighty-five years ago. Europe is mostly at peace today, a condition it didn't enjoy for centuries up until the Allied victory in 1945. Even in places such as the former Soviet Union that have not fully eradicated the old tyrannies, the circumstances of life are much improved over even two decades ago. China is not a free country, but memories of the harsh experiences of the Mao years have been buried by more than three decades of dramatic capitalistic economic growth. Viable democracies have emerged in Chile, Colombia, and Peru, not to mention the onetime Soviet satellite states.

It would be hard to imagine what the people of Whiteland, circa 1933, would have thought about the rich and scientifically advanced twenty-first century America. But there is some reason to think that they might have had a better visceral understanding than do many Americans today of why America has prospered. Today's wealth and creature comforts are sometimes taken for granted, with little thought to how they came about. Perhaps the people of our Indiana village better understood the fundamentals of economic development because they had little inherited wealth and had to depend upon their own resourcefulness. They knew that they had to produce something of value to survive, and fortunately they had the freedom to exercise and exploit their own ideas.

In short, they knew instinctively something that the great economic philosopher John Stuart Mill had written in 1844: "What a country wants to make it richer, is never consumption, but production." Production was the primary challenge of life. That key point seems to have gotten lost in the Washington of the 1930s, which unwisely and sometimes unwittingly constrained production and intensely focused on "consumption." It is still not clearly understood by many thinkers and policy makers in academia and government today.

What Hoover and the New Dealers saw as a problem of "overproduction" was actually a distortion of efficient resource allocation—meaning land, labor, and capital put to its most valued uses—brought about by various kinds of government interventions, including subsidized farm loans and other forms of manipulation of the credit markets. This sort of intervention is very much with us today in the form of the near-zero interest rates artificially induced by the Fed and which facilitated the massive federal borrowing that doubled the national debt in a mere seven years, from fiscal years 2007 to 2014, adding $9 trillion.

Combined with this distortion has been an enormous expansion of government restraints on production. Wayne Crews of the Competitive Enterprise Institute in Washington every year compiles what he calls the "Ten Thousand Commandments," a compilation of government regulations and what he estimates to be their costs to the economy. He estimated that in 2013 it cost Americans more than $1.8 trillion to comply with federal regulations, an average of almost $15,000 per household, or 29 percent of total household expenditures. Small businesses had higher compliance costs per employee on average than large ones, $10,585 for firms with fewer than twenty workers, versus $7,755 for those with five hundred or more.

The 2013 *Federal Register*, which lists all new laws and rules put forth by those of the government's 435 agencies authorized to independently issue regulations, had 79,311 pages in 2013. That rivaled the all-time record of 81,405 in 2010, the year Obamacare and the Dodd-Frank banking act became law.

Modern official puzzlement over why the economy isn't growing faster is reminiscent of the 1930s. The government today is focused on promoting consumption, while at the same time suppressing production. There is a certain resemblance here to the artificial efforts of Hoover and Roosevelt to maintain consumption, some of them, as in the case of FDR's NRA "buy now" cheerleading, rather silly sounding. The rediscovery of Mill's simple observation might be very useful in coping with the economic uncertainties that afflict us. If you have an income, consumption comes naturally and is only limited by prudent budgeting. Production, on the other hand, requires work and imagination.

One might say that that awesome word *economics*, so much bandied about in political debate, is best understood in its simplest terms as a study of human work effort and creativity as people set about to make a living, get ahead, and achieve a higher standard of security and comfort. All the scientific mumbo jumbo of modern mathematical economics, or econometrics, is fine so far as it goes in examining transactional complexities, but if you want to think about it in its simplest terms you might consider that at bottom the "the economy" is nothing more nor less than the sum total of human work effort.

My observation, certainly not original with me or even with Ronald Reagan, is that government policies work best when they don't inhibit this natural dynamic. Some of what are called "social" policies of the 1930s may have contributed to that dynamic in that they have socialized risk, meaning that some of the risks undertaken or encountered by individuals were underwritten by the larger society.

Arguably, providing a better safety net for risk takers encourages the more chancy investments of time and money that open up new frontiers and lead to economic advancement. But it wouldn't do to carry that argument too far because it might begin to sound like a defense for government-provided corporate welfare, which distorts the efficient allocation of resources. There is, however, an argument for providing individuals with some level of protection against adversity, on humanitarian grounds at the very least.

The limiting factor here is that at some point the socialization of risk can become too expensive for the larger polity to sustain, and it thus becomes counterproductive. The United States may be close to reaching that point. "Old Age, Survivors, and Disability Insurance," better known as Social Security, was legislated by the New Deal in 1935 and fits the safety net category. It had a wide range of political support, including from business organizations such as the National Association of Manufacturers.

Certainly it had flaws, including the deliberately misleading description of the program as "insurance" when it was in fact a generational income transfer from the working-age population to the elderly. True insurance policies, as issued by private companies like Metropolitan Life, are funded by premiums invested in ways that produce a return. The Social Security "fund" consists only of a huge batch of nonnegotiable IOUs held by the government itself, which are hardly "funds" in the accepted sense but obligations assigned to future tax-payers.

The elderly men and women of Whiteland, excepting farmers who were excluded, welcomed its advent. Their el-derly descendants guard it jealously and even resist the mod-ifications that will have to come eventually if the huge burden of supporting the national debt is to be prevented from crowding out the government's spending for all other needs, including national defense.

CHAPTER TWENTY-EIGHT

★

THE PROGRESSIVES

No DISCUSSION OF the 1930s and the New Deal would be complete without some mention of the progressive movement in America. One might say that the movement was a political expression of Newton's Third Law: "For every action there is an equal and opposite reaction." In the nineteenth century, tycoons like Andrew Carnegie and John D. Rockefeller had built large private business organizations employing thousands of workers. On a local scale, James T. Polk's Greenwood canning factory and dairy were examples of this kind of private enterprise, which in fact was the propelling force behind the nation's burgeoning business and industrial infrastructure development in the nineteenth and twentieth centuries.

The progressives had a suspicion of and an antipathy toward private empire builders, dubbing them "robber barons" and the like. They thought these "trusts" should be brought under better government control, so that their behavior would correspond to the broad public interest, rather than just the interests of their owners. That view found purchase among voters, and a progressive politician, Republican Theodore Roosevelt, was elected in a landslide in his own right in 1904. The charismatic, hyperactive "Teddy" already had served three years after moving up from vice president with the 1901 assassination of President William McKinley.

Excoriating "enormously wealthy and economically powerful men," a theme that has a familiar ring even today, Teddy had set out early to bring the corporations to heel by filing forty antitrust suits against them. He succeeded in breaking up one of the largest companies, Rockefeller's Standard Oil Company, into smaller, more localized corporate units. That success was based on the argument that Standard was a vicious monopoly. The fact that Standard Oil's efficiency and economies of scale had actually sharply reduced the price of kerosene, a product used by just about every American to light lamps in the nineteenth century, didn't spare it from progressive wrath.

That there were corporate abuses of their power, no one could doubt. "Teddy" focused on the sanitation shortcomings of the food packing industry, meatpackers in particular, and won passage of the Pure Food and Drug Act, which exercises powerful control over the food and drug industry to this day.

When the Republican Party decided it had had enough of Teddy in 1912 and denied him the nomination in favor of the steadier incumbent, William Howard Taft, he created his own progressive party, dubbing it the Bull Moose Party, and split the Republican vote, enabling Democrat Woodrow Wilson, a former president of Princeton University, to become president. But progressivism remained an important current in American politics and reemerged in 1932 as a powerful force within the New Deal, a name that awakened memories of what Teddy had called his "square deal." Indeed, Franklin Roosevelt was Teddy's fifth cousin.

Some progressives were so antibusiness that they went so far as to look for alternatives to private capitalism. One of the "muckrakers" who had attacked corporations in the early twentieth century was the journalist Lincoln Steffens, a writer for *McClure's Magazine*. He was granted a guided tour of the newly formed Soviet Union in 1919, only a year after the Bolshevik overthrow of the Kerensky government, Russia's failed attempt to form a post-czarist republic. On his return, Steffens uttered a line in an address to an American Soviet support group that would be famously recorded as "I have seen the future and it works" (some recollections phrase it "I have been over into the future," etc., but the meaning is the same).

The Soviet experiment in fashioning an economy centrally planned and controlled by a powerful government would fascinate American intellectuals for years thereafter. Joseph Stalin, who had ambitions to expand Russian imperialism when he came to power in 1924, would capitalize on that fascination. He invited other American leaders and intellectuals to come to Russia to be impressed by the collectivist Potemkin villages he had created. One tourist was a Washington bureaucrat named Stuart Chase, who in 1927 was a member of a trade union delegation. He wrote a book praising Stalin's experiments in the socialization of farming and other industries, titling it *A New Deal*. Either by accident or the design of FDR speechwriter Sam Rosenman, the term found its way into FDR's 1932 speech accepting the presidency and thereafter became the historical description of his revolutionary explosion of statist legislation.

Another graduate of a Soviet guided tour was Columbia professor Rexford Tugwell. He, too, was impressed with the claimed efficacy of the central planning practiced by the Russians. That view would find its way into the 1933 Agricultural Adjustment Act, which he played a major role in designing, not to mention his grand designs for resettling millions of Americans into government-planned communities.

The guileful Stalin was adept at charming impressionable would-be reformers like Chase and Tugwell. He also had great success with Walter Duranty, a *New York Times* reporter who was one of the few foreign journalists allowed to cover the Soviet experiment. Stalin turned Duranty's head by drawing him into his inner circle, giving him access that he could boast about to his editors in New York.

What Duranty didn't have access to was the big story that Stalin did not want revealed, his use of tyranny to create the utopia that his fellow Marxist theoreticians had imagined. In particular, Duranty missed the mass deaths from starvation of the Ukrainian farmers uprooted from their land to create the collective farms that so impressed visitors like Chase and Tugwell.

Other writers and intellectuals with an antipathy toward capitalism would have resonance in the troubled 1930s, unable to recognize that the radical economic interventions of the New Deal government might be making things worse rather than better for the nation's poor and underrepresented.

One was the California author John Steinbeck. His novel *The Grapes of Wrath* depicted the desperately poor fictional Joad farm family migrating from the Oklahoma Dust Bowl to a California that didn't welcome them. The talents of director John Ford and actors Jane Darwell and Henry Fonda turned the story of the Joads into a touching blockbuster of a movie.

It was a type of a literature, common at the time, that blamed "the system" for the hardship depicted, implying that the "system," usually meaning free-market capitalism, was a form of oppression by the rich and powerful and thus required the drastic change that only a more forceful government could bring about. A Wikipedia entry quotes Steinbeck, who won Pulitzer and Nobel prizes for his work, as having said, "I want to put a tag of shame on the greedy bastards who are responsible for this [the Great Depression and its effects]." He famously said, "I've done my damndest to rip a reader's nerves to rags."

In 1939, when *Grapes* was published, it was not hard to tear the reader's nerves to shreds, but that was after a decade not of greedy capitalism but of failed government experiments in economic policy. Steinbeck didn't make the connection. He seemed to think that California farm owners were the "greedy bastards" and so he failed to give the government any blame for the long period of hard times. The New Deal had been in power for more than six years when his novel was published and had not been a timid exercise of government power.

Steinbeck also didn't give sufficient credit to the weather for the hardship of some farmers like the fictional Joads. Drought afflicted large parts of the country west of the Alleghenies in the years 1934–37, creating the Dust Bowl in Oklahoma, the Texas Panhandle, and parts of New Mexico and Kansas. Tillage of the thin topsoil over the years had made farms vulnerable to extended drought. Dust storms were the result when winds whipped up the dried-out land. Farms just blew away.

The Midwest was also affected by the droughts in 1934 and 1936, dealing the farmers there a bittersweet experience in the form of low crop yields but significantly higher commodity prices. Summer nights in 1936 were so hot that some of us in Whiteland took our mattresses outside to get a cooler sleep.

At any rate, the supposed migration of masses of "Arkie" and "Okie" farmers to California was greatly exaggerated. Only a few thousand made the arduous long-distance move, later census studies showed. Most of the migrants went no farther than neighboring states. To be sure, a lot of Americans, especially nonfarmers, headed for California in the 1930s, but that was because better opportunities existed there than in the East, South, and Midwest.

Spokesmen for the Associated Farmers of California were exceedingly angered at the way farmers were depicted in the Steinbeck novel as cruel and callous in their treatment of the migrants in camps that had been set up to house farmworkers. They accused Steinbeck of having painted them that way to make a political point. Do tell! Steinbeck in his writings had a special animus toward property owners and there's little doubt that he was interested in scoring political points.

Steinbeck's attack on California farm owners followed in the tradition of another prominent author of the era, Sinclair Lewis. Lewis felt compelled to heap scorn on small-town boosterism, especially in his 1922 book, *Babbitt,* based roughly on his remembrances of the Chamber of Commerce types in his hometown of Sauk Center, Minnesota. His portraits of hinterland hicks won him praise from sophisticates in New York's literary salons.

Neither Lewis nor Steinbeck was a profound thinker, but urban liberals liked their assaults on rural or small-town achievers. They were loath to acknowledge that men and women who had built profitable businesses were the bedrock of the American economy and the dedicated preservers of social mores that were widely accepted and had formed a social bond among residents of small communities. The Lewis form of social snobbery didn't go down well in places like Whiteland, Greenwood, and Franklin, small towns that owed much of the wealth they possessed to the ambition and energy of their Babbitts.

Steinbeck's *Grapes* message of capitalist tyranny fit well with the politics of the New Deal, even though it must have occurred to some readers that the hardships he was framing were occurring *after* the New Deal had launched its revolutionary antipoverty measures. Franklin Roosevelt and his politically active wife, Eleanor, adopted Steinbeck as one of their favorites and as a demonstration that they, too, despite their upper-class upbringings, had the interests of the common man at heart. No doubt that feeling was genuine, particularly with Eleanor, even if the New Deal's actual policies bore little fruit for the plebeian types who lived ordinary lives in places like Whiteland. Noblesse oblige doesn't put bread on the table.

The Works Projects Administration (WPA) "writers project" subsidized many writers who shared the Steinbeck point of view. Some might say—and some historians indeed have—that the project was set up simply because FDR and his associates had a special affection for writers, as opposed to, say, window washers. But there was little evidence that the writing profession needed or deserved greater support from government than any other livelihood. Good books were being written by writers not on the government dole and there was no shortage of reading matter.

The WPA was a political project under political management and it's not totally unbelievable that some of the policy makers could see political advantages in winning the favor of people who had the skills to influence public opinion. One also could argue, perhaps unkindly but with some justification, that some New Dealers were not only influenced by the experiments in central economic planning being conducted across the Atlantic, but were also learning lessons from Europe in the art of capturing the intellectual class and putting it to their own uses.

Whitelanders were no different from anyone else in feeling the influence of this kind of politics. After all, someone has to be blamed for adversity, and who better than the fat, top-hatted malefactors of great wealth portrayed in editorial

cartoons in your local newspaper. A perceptive widely syndicated newspaper columnist of the 1930s, Walter Lippmann,
observed that primitive societies attributed their troubles to
an "evil eye." Americans blamed Wall Street. Lippmann was
no right-winger. He knew FDR well but was a frequent critic
of New Deal excesses. His ultimate assessment: FDR was a
great wartime leader, but a failure at domestic policy.

CHAPTER TWENTY-NINE

WHITELAND TODAY

THE OLD WHITELAND is long gone. Housing developments have raised its population tenfold, to 4,300. Shoppers long ago abandoned its general stores for big-box emporiums like the Walmart southward on the now-four-lane Highway 31, or Meijer over on the broad and busy state Highway 135, which my mother once called the three-notch road. The grain elevator and the coal yard, Harry Porter's drugstore, the Thompson Hotel, Fishers' store, and the old bank building disappeared ages ago. There's no sign of where Stokely's or the brick factory once stood. "Downtown" was recently a motor home sales lot.

The one-story brick building that once was the business center still stands but recently housed a graphics firm.

There's now a city hall, an expanded post office, and a small Pleasant Township office offering social services. The original Whiteland schoolhouse is gone. The school and its administrative office building are the most prominent features of what used to be a town sprinkled with small businesses. There are small shops on U.S. 31, some on the site where our grocery store once stood, part of a string of small businesses that line the highway from Indianapolis to Franklin. One recent one was a tattoo parlor. The Interurban was shut down at the beginning of World War II and no trace remains. Suburban bus service has been discontinued as well. There's a recreational raceway north of town where people can have fun driving small, low-powered cars around a winding track.

Greenwood has changed more dramatically, although it retains more of its old downtown identity than Whiteland. The intersection of Main and Madison looks familiar, with some of the same buildings that stood there in the 1930s. There are still descendants of old families in both Whiteland and Greenwood, such as the Brewers, McClains, or Myers.

But Greenwood is a very different place. It years ago annexed White River Township, now the site of upmarket housing developments. Its population today is nearly 50,000, compared to the 2,300 of the 1930s. Greenwood Park, a large indoor shopping mall, has in recent years housed Macy's, Nordstrom, Sears, and dozens of other outlets. Greenwood Airport, where the Wheatcraft boys once taught young men and women to fly Piper Cubs, now hangars dozens of modern aircraft. Its five-thousand-foot paved runway can accommodate medium-size jets. The total assessed value of Greenwood property is more than $2 billion.

Greenwood is not even the richest suburb of Indianapolis. The really snazzy places, like Carmel, are on the north side. Today's America has thousands of rich suburbs that were once distinct—and usually distinctly poor—little villages scattered throughout farmlands from which men like Roy Sharp once eked out a small living for their families. Testimony to the large growth in discretionary income can be found in the form of numerous service establishments that in the 1930s would been regarded as frivolous had they existed, such as nail manicure salons or pet grooming establishments.

Huge dealerships on Highways 31 and 135 selling new cars and trucks have supplanted the little in-town showrooms of Kelly Motors–type vendors of the 1930s. The small downtown cafés of yesteryear have given way to dozens of busy franchise restaurants catering to a population with plenty of dining-out money. The ramps of Interstate 65 ingest and debouch streams of cars and trucks. The trip from Louisville to Whiteland, which cost my father an uncomfortable week of travel by horse and wagon, can now be made by car in an hour and a half.

I witnessed a sign of the more cosmopolitan nature of once-rural places at a Greenwood Fourth of July parade a few years ago. Among all the traditional floats of the Jaycees, Kiwanis, Rotary, and local auto dealers was one with beautiful Chinese décor carrying pretty, costumed, young Chinese women. They were handing out flyers for Falun Gong, the organization devoted to traditional meditative exercises and which the Beijing government set about to suppress in 1999. The movement's members, facing arrest in their homeland, have internationalized their practices and resistance to the continued authoritarianism of Beijing.

There are thousands of towns like Greenwood that have blossomed out of small villages and have grown wealthy in a single lifetime. This is the unique way that such things happen in America. One would think that the ability of its people to keep free market private capitalism alive in the face of constant challenges had something to do with that.

Market capitalism survived the series of experiments of economic planners and social engineers in the 1930s thanks in part to the Supreme Court's strong-willed adherence to the U.S. Constitution's defined limits on the powers of the federal government. That document does not give a president, even one as charming as FDR, dictatorial powers. Capitalism's survival was aided by the spectacular demonstration of private sector vitality in the mobilization for World War II and in the postwar revival of the economies of the defeated powers Germany and Japan. Finally, it survived because market capitalism, through which millions of private citizens make millions of decisions daily in service of their own best interests, is incredibly resistant to the natural tendency of governments to expand their reach and power.

The capitalist structure has been greatly modified by evolution of management attitudes and practices in large business corporations. They are now run, on the whole, by well-educated, well-paid professionals, rather than by often-untutored storekeepers and mechanics who founded them years ago and continued as owner-operators. Their once-narrow ownership is now very broad, thanks to the many millions of Americans who are beneficial owners through mutual funds and pension programs. Corporations, especially banks, are far more heavily regulated by government—sometimes for better but too often for worse. But all these modifications aside, it is still market capitalism.

The nation's demographics have changed dramatically with the evolution of an urban culture replacing the highly decentralized agrarian society of the 1930s. But after all these years, the fundamental genes of that old order are still embedded in the DNA of Americans. We still treasure economic freedom and admire the innovations that improve the quality of life. The wonders of the 1920s were automobiles that could do 40 miles per hour and all-metal passenger airplanes attaining speeds of more than 150 miles per hour. Today's wonders are things like heart transplants, Google searches that can pull any one of billions of facts out of the ether in a fraction of a second, a space probe that has already exited our solar system, and GPS systems equipped with the voices of nice ladies who tell you to turn right at the next corner.

It's important to keep these enormous differences in mind when trying to evaluate the politics and economic policies of the Depression era. But recalling the mistakes of the past is nonetheless useful in reviewing the policies of the present.

The traditional explanation of America's rise to wealth and international political preeminence may seem like a cliché to sophisticated ears, but sometimes thoughts become clichés because of their fundamental validity. Who can refute that all this came about because of the ability of private individuals to protect their property rights, economic freedom, access to an honest judiciary, and ability to choose their leaders by means of regularly scheduled and reasonably fair elections? Those circumstances have not been available to most peoples of the world, but even where they exist only in part, such as a China that now has its own version of market capitalism, there has been progress.

The change from the 1930s has been spectacular. A factory worker living in Whiteland today has more comforts, conveniences, and protections against illness than Franklin D. Roosevelt or England's King George VI had in 1933. He can be treated with lifesaving drugs and surgical procedures at modern medical centers, like the new St. Francis Hospital, that have proliferated in the Indianapolis area. In 1933, we didn't even have penicillin. When he becomes infirm, he can probably wangle access to a modern nursing home with Medicaid paying most of the bill.

The great, late economist Julian Simon totted up America's advances in a 1996 paper called "The Ultimate Resource," a defense of liberal immigration policies on the grounds that population growth goes hand in hand with economic advancement.

He calculated that the average American at the time of his writing had available ten times more miles of paved roads than in the 1920s; almost twice as many physicians, the quality of which was incalculably higher; 50 percent more dentists, also of incalculably greater skill; three times as many teachers; close to six times as many police officers; about twice as many firefighters; and the production of about two and a half times more cubic feet of lumber even as the size of lumber stands in the United States also increased.

And, perhaps most important, each American worker had about 8.5 times more capital equipment to work with. That means that every industrial worker is far more productive than in the days when Walter Thomas, Bart Whitney, and I were digging ditches by hand and Roy Sharp had to hitch up a team of horses to his primitive farm implements and spend many hours in the fields to raise crops.

Certainly further gains have been made since 1996. That's why food products, after adjustments for decades of inflation, are cheaper than eighty years ago in terms of the work hours needed to buy them. Appliances like electric toasters or coffee machines are sold at a fraction of their costs when they first came on the market years ago. This opulence didn't happen in a vacuum. It needed air to breathe.

Progressivism staged a comeback after the 2008–9 financial debacle. It was dubbed the "Great Recession" to indicate that it was not as bad as the "Great Depression," but nonetheless "Great," so pardon us in Washington if our remedies don't seem to be working very well. As in 1929–30, government had a great deal to do with bringing about the recession and its remedies a great deal to do with prolonging its effects.

In the old days it was Hoover's taxes and tariffs and FDR's efforts to rearrange the entire American economy and place it under government management that caused trouble. In modern times it was the creation of many billions of dollars of subprime mortgages to satisfy federal "affordable housing" policies. Government-sponsored mortgage buyers and insurers Fannie Mae and Freddie Mac issued securities backed by these shaky mortgages that were bought by banks and investors all over the world. When the housing price bubble began to deflate in 2006, it exposed the fact that many homeowners had little or no equity and could easily walk away from their homes and mortgage payments. Securities backed by these distressed mortgages became "toxic" and many banks holding them, required by law to mark them to market value, found themselves illiquid. When big Lehman Brothers crashed so did stock markets.

Just as the 1929 crash brought to power the progressives, who of course blamed Wall Street, the 2008 crash brought a new generation of progressives into control of Congress and the presidency under the leadership of Barack Obama. As in 1933, they were not about to let a good crisis go to waste. In 1933, we got the revolutionary AAA and NIRA, both declared unconstitutional by the Supreme Court. In 2010, we got the Affordable Care Act (ACA), a massive federal rearrangement and control of the health insurance and health care industry, also with serious constitutional problems. A new banking act granted unprecedented powers to the U.S. Treasury and Federal Reserve to supervise the financial sector.

In 1933, the Federal Reserve clearly was implicated in the causes of the Depression. In 2008, it can be argued, it overreacted to fears that the crash might send the monetary system into another deflationary spiral of the type that occurred seventy-five years earlier. It dropped interest rates to near zero, distorting the credit market against savers and pension funds and in favor of heavy federal borrowing and a doubling of the national debt.

It can be plausibly argued that the expansion of government power over economic processes, often encouraged by lobbyists seeking competitive advantage, as in years past, has loaded the economy with unneeded and wasteful regulation. Farmers brought about their own undoing in 1933 with the Smoot-Hawley tariffs and the AAA. Large health insurance firms did the same in their support for the ACA, better known as Obamacare, and are now suffering buyers' remorse.

Syndicated columnist George Will wrote on February 4, 2015, that more than six years after the 2008 crash, the American economy was still weak and that the "anemia was an iatrogenic social ailment, induced by government behavior." (I had to look up that fancy word *iatrogenic*; it means an illness caused by the treatment.) Will wrote that the business burdens and uncertainties created by the Affordable Care Act were just part of the Obama administration's regulatory mania, citing Wayne Crew's finding of 3,659 new regulations finalized in 2013 and the 2,594 others proposed. New business formations were at a thirty-five-year low. He cited estimates that in a normal recovery the United States would have had "15 million more jobs than it had at the end of 2014."

The United States, even though still ranked by Freedom House as a free country, has lost ground. It has slipped to twelfth place by last count on the annual *Wall Street Journal/* Heritage Foundation Index of Economic Freedom. The trend is toward further erosion. This may account for the surprisingly high level of voter discontent and thus support for mavericks like Donald Trump and socialist Bernie Sanders at the outset of the 2016 presidential campaign.

Voters and politicians might want to take a fresh look at the neo-Keynesian theory that government has the power to "stimulate" consumption through easy money and heavy federal spending. That theory has again been tested as it was in the 1930s and found wanting.

It is sometimes forgotten that Herbert Hoover's response to the 1929 crash was a large program of public works spending and that his policy was continued by FDR. None of that was very effective in restoring economic vitality after the crashes of 1929 and 1937. Serial trillion-dollar federal deficits coupled with the Fed's near-zero interest rates didn't prove very effective in pulling the economy out of the modern "Great Recession," either. As nearly as one can tell, the reason seems to have been in both cases that government actions created uncertainties and actual barriers to investment that undermined public confidence and thus the willingness to make bets on the future.

Like the NRA's puerile messages urging consumers to spend, so-called consumption measures by government are usually a costly sideshow. It doesn't take much intelligence to understand that we all want to enjoy higher living standards, which for some might mean frequent champagne dinners or a new Mercedes. For others, as with Eliza Doolittle of *My Fair Lady,* just "a room somewhere far away from the cold night air" might be a step upward. Surely, we don't need government to urge us to satisfy our wants. What we need is wherewithal. To get it, as would surely be the case for most of us, we need to produce or help produce something with marketable value.

It isn't likely that Liberia is a poor country because its citizens have no desire to consume, one might guess. Probably they would consume far more if they had more money. Most likely they're poor because deficiencies in education and years of corrupt government have suppressed creativity and left them with only a limited ability to produce marketable goods, the sale of which would earn them the wherewithal to consume more and lead more comfortable and healthy lives.

Entrepreneurs in my country village understood what might be called supply-side economics ninety years ago without ever having heard the term, or for that matter, much of the language of modern economics. Compared to today, they were subject to very little official restraint of their ability to find ways to make a living. There were few licensing requirements to practice a trade. If you wanted to start a business you just did, and if you wanted to incorporate it, it was simply a matter of filling out a few forms and paying a small fee.

What might be called a natural order was to be thrown into disarray, I have argued, when advocates of more extensive and intrusive government economic management came to power. Life would never be the same afterward, for better and for worse, but in the 1930s and again in our modern era, it was mostly for worse.

IT TAKES A VILLAGE . . .

IN A POPULAR 1947 song titled "That's What I Like About the South," singer-band leader Phil Harris sings fondly about a place called "Doo Wye Ditty" that was "awfully small but awfully pretty." My home village was awfully small and not really what I would call pretty. But many of us who grew up there seemed to have a particularly warm sense of nostalgia when we think about the Whiteland of yore.

Hugh Jackson Ross's little book is full of such warm reminiscences, such as an admiring recollection of how pretty

Ruth Lorrene Jones used to deliver the *Franklin Evening Star*, folding the papers into neat squares while she was riding her bicycle and pitching them accurately onto front porches with nary a pause. Ruth Lorrene was an orphan girl who supported herself and her indigent grandmother by delivering papers in late afternoon and assisting John Dickson, the school janitor, with cleaning blackboards and sweeping floors late into the night, then getting up the next morning to go to school. She dealt with the difficulties of her life with competence and good cheer.

According to the conventional narrative, life for almost everyone in America during the Great Depression was pretty miserable. But country girl Carolyn Wendt, daughter of Roy Sharp, said not long ago, "We had a wonderful childhood!" I thought so, too, but I am aware that some of our contemporaries weren't as fortunate.

"It takes a village to raise a child" was the theme of a 1996 book written by then–first lady Hillary Clinton (with some help from ghostwriter Barbara Feinman), drawing on what was said to be an African proverb, the origins of which has proved elusive to scholars. Critics argued that Clinton was extolling the beauties of communal living. Perhaps that's an unfair characterization of her views, but it's true that her Democratic political party has had egalitarian collectivist leanings since the New Deal, whereas the Republicans, in their rhetoric at least, have more often cheered for individualism.

There have been some interesting but impermanent collectives in American history. Examples were the nineteenth-century Shaker villages in several eastern states and an early-nineteenth-century utopian village called New Harmony, on the Wabash River in southwestern Indiana, organized along socialist lines in 1825 by Welsh industrialist Robert Owen. Utopian villages never caught on in America and indeed utopianism has a rather bad name today after the communal ideal proved to be a disguise for tyranny in places like Russia and China in the twentieth century. The idea has worked best in Israel, where mostly Eastern European Jewish immigrants established communal villages (kibbutzim) beginning in 1909 that have lasted more than a century.

Whiteland was only a hundred miles from New Harmony, now a tourist attraction, but a far cry from any communal ideal. Children were mostly well cared for by their families but they didn't get, or seemingly need, much nurturing from the townfolk. We were merely tolerated when noticed at all as we helped with household chores and entertained ourselves with pickup ball games, playing Monopoly, shooting at targets with BB guns, building model airplanes, or exploring country roads on our bicycles, sometimes riding out to Bert Meredith's gravel pit to skinny-dip. Most adults had too many other fish to fry than to worry about nurturing the town's younger generation. By and large, we had a free-range upbringing.

But if Clinton was intending to convey a broader sense of the opportunities in a small community of learning about the ways of the world, she had a point. My little farm village offered a greater familiarity with the variety of people around us and, for that matter, more gossip about their comings and goings, than might have been available to a child in an urban area. Growing up in hard times that would segue into war meant that we came of age in a particularly meaningful period of history.

Farm-village life in an agrarian era when a large proportion of Americans lived in farm towns or on the farms themselves offered a small window through which to view the realities of the early 1930s firsthand. That view provided a glimpse of how the individualistic, entrepreneurial people of an era when most Americans made their living from small businesses proved their resilience in coping with adversity.

Perhaps growing up in a village was an antidote to the danger of treating an electorate, or the readers of a newspaper, as an amorphous mass, as in the "great proletarian masses" referred to by the Bolsheviks. We were few in number, but that only emphasized the degree to which we were all individuals, each enjoying in our ways that great gift, life itself, and each with his own sense of identity and his own set of preferences. Some of us thought General Motors made the best cars. Others liked Fords, or Plymouths. Some of us went to church on Sundays. Some didn't. Some thought FDR was a savior of the nation. Others hated him. The beauty lay in the fact that we had a choice. The intimacy of a small community taught us to recognize and respect differences and to distrust absolutism. We were all free Americans and thus entitled to be the persons we chose to be within the informal bounds of the mores of the community and our own capacities.

That view of the world suggests that we should treat our leaders and their mistakes with some charity. They, too, are individuals, with their own sense of identity and their own visions of what constitutes a just society. Their motives for what they do might be complicated, and in some cases may include an element of a lust for power, opportunism, or cupidity. But representative government also makes them mindful of the interests of their constituencies, however limited or poorly defined. When they have misjudged, it often has been with the conception in their minds that their intentions were good.

But a good general rule for the people of a representative government is to not grant leaders more power than they can handle or to vote for candidates who promise too much. They are only mere humans. When tempted to say, "There ought to be a law," reconsider. Maybe there shouldn't be a law. Maybe we would all be better off if there were a lot fewer laws than we have now. On that score, the people of the village may have been better off than we are today under the rule of "progressive" government.

As to where we go from here, there's that old saying that the hardest thing to predict is the future. It's hard enough even to gain some understanding of the past, as the many varied theories of what caused the Great Depression—including those I have just written—attest. But on the whole, the past has been good to America. Its guiding political and legal principles have served it well. One hopes that the DNA we inherited will continue to sustain us.

ACKNOWLEDGMENTS

MY SINCEREST THANKS to my Whiteland school classmate Carolyn Wendt for sharing the memories of life on the farm that are an important part of this book. I also must remember all those whose genealogical research was indispensable. They include my late sister, Marie Randolph of Franklin, Indiana, and my late cousin, David Melloan, of Lawrenceburg, Kentucky. The prodigious family history files of another cousin, Susan Thorpe, a Leitchfield, Kentucky, artist, also were immensely useful.

Finally, I must thank my family. My son, Jim, applied his magazine editing skills to clean up the manuscript. Maryanne, a TV scriptwriter and playwright, provided assurance through her interest in my early life that this was a worthwhile project. Her husband and daughter, Johnny and Sara Woods, gave moral support. Molly, who once illustrated my *Wall Street Journal* columns, made a major contribution by decorating this book with her drawings. My niece, Cathy Melloan, provided image research.

And I honor the memory of my late wife, Joan, whose journalistic talents and love of writing were a constant source of inspiration during our many years together. I dedicate this book to her.

INDEX

blacksmith shop (Whiteland), 5, 114
blue eagle (NRA symbol), 149, 150, 174
Boone family, 84
bootleg alcohol, 9, 59, 115
Bretton Woods monetary system, 191
Brewer family, 210
Bridgeport Brass Corporation, 162, 179
Brisbane, Arthur, 143
Brokaw, Tom, 192
Brown, Brendan, 42
Brown, Hattie and Lee, 76–77
Brunnemer, "Link," 100
Brunnemer, Myron, 52, 53
Brunnemer, Winifred "Wimp," 100
business/corporations
    confidence in, 156, 170, 171
    Coolidge and, 112–13
    cooperation of labor, government and,
        32, 149
    FDR and, 48–49, 169, 172, 184, 194
    foreign, 173
    Hoover and, 26, 31, 32–33, 194
    and housing for women, 120
    human relations departments at, 173
    and modifications of capitalism,
        212–13
    ownership of, 212–13
    in post–World War II years, 189, 191
    progressives and, 200–201, 202
    regulation of, 196–97, 213
    Republicans as friendly toward, 26
    resilience of, 224
    and role of government in economy,
        27
    small, 112–17, 196, 210, 224
    taxes on, 124–26, 170
    and wages, 32
    World War II and, 162, 180–81,
        184–85
    See also National Recovery
        Administration (NRA); specific
        legislation
butter/oleomargarine, 29
"buy now," 151, 152, 197

California: migration to, 67, 205
Camp Atterbury, 185
canning, 118–26, 175–77. See also specific
    factory
capitalism, 189–90, 191, 193, 195, 202, 204,
    212–13, 214. See also free market
"car line," Interurban, 2–3, 78, 163–64, 165,
    210
Carnegie, Andrew, 200
carnival troupe, Scott's, 7–8, 79
cars
    cost of, 102–3
    cross-country trips in, 63–68

in early twentieth century, 107
and individualism, 224
as means for adventure, 63–64
Melloan (Bob) love of, 59–60
and Melloan (Connie) at car crash,
    61–62
of Melloan family, 1, 2, 4, 22, 60
in 1920s, 59–60
ownership of, 114
and quality of life, 213
racing, 102
steering on, 67
See also automobile industry
cattle trading, 22–23
Chalmers car, 22, 59–60
charity. See relief agencies
Chase National Bank, 38
Chase, Stuart, 149, 203
Chevrolet Motor Company, 97–98
China, 155, 193, 195, 211–12, 214, 223
churches, 81, 83–84. See also specific church
Clinton, Hillary, 168, 222, 223
coal, 92, 93–94, 95, 98–99, 109, 152, 209
cobbler shop (Whiteland), 4, 75, 114
Columbia Club (Indianapolis), 58
communes/collectives, 222–23
Communications Workers of America v. Beck
    (1988), 141–42
communism, 190–91
Community House (Greenwood), 87
competition, 29, 98, 100–101, 150, 152, 160
Competitive Enterprise Institute, 196
Conference Board, 126
Congress of Industrial Organizations (CIO),
    169, 171, 172
Congress, U.S.
    Democratic control of, 35, 47
    elections of 1932 and, 47
    and gold standard, 137
    "one hundred days" of legislation
        by, 49
    and presidential powers, 49
    See also Democrats; Republicans;
        specific legislation
Constitution, U.S., 9, 49, 59, 138, 146, 152,
    212, 216
consumers/consumption
    and AAA, 145
    and "buy now," 151, 152, 197
    and cause of Great Depression, 38
    focus on, 196, 197, 218–19
    and "Greatest Generation," 195–96
    Hoover policies and, 32
    and productivity, 219
    and role of government in economy,
        218–19
    spending by, 218–19
    See also deflation; inflation; prices

St. Louis: Whiteland town boys trip to, 104
Stalin, Joseph, xii, 149, 186, 190, 202–3
Standard Oil Company, 201
Standard Oil of Indiana, 81
Standard Red Crown pump, 76
steel industry, 171, 172, 173, 190
Steffens, Lincoln, 202
Steinbeck, John, 204–7
"stimulus" spending, 37
stock market, 41, 139, 216. *See also specific crash*
Stokely canning factory, 5, 78, 110, 123, 124, 145, 151–52, 157, 158, 167, 175, 178, 179, 209
Stokely family, 123, 145, 157, 174, 175, 176, 178, 179, 209
Stokely Van Camp, 179
Stoner, Charles S., 115–17
Strong, Benjamin, 45–46
subprime mortgages, 215–16
subsidies, for farmers, 55–56, 143, 144, 145, 147, 196
Supreme Court, U.S., 138, 141–42, 146, 152–53, 156, 212, 216
Swope, Gerard, 32, 150

Taft, William Howard, 202
Tariff Act (1930), 33–35, 140, 217
tariffs, 30, 33–35, 215
Tax Court, U.S., 124
taxes, 35–37, 124–26, 170, 171, 190, 215
teachers, 177, 214–15
technology, 80, 147, 213
"Ten Thousand Commandments," 196–97
Tennessee Valley Authority (TVA), 36
Thomas, Elmer, 145–46
Thomas, Walter, 162, 215
Thompson, Dorothy Jean. *See* Melloan, Dorothy Jean Thompson
Thompson Hotel (Whiteland), 4, 75, 158, 209
Thompson, "Jack," 159
threshing machines, 51
threshing rings, 50–54, 142
tomatoes, 119–20, 121–22, 123–24, 125, 167, 175–76, 177, 178, 185–86
tonsils: removal of, 62
Townsend, Clifford, 169
tractors, 52–53
trade, 11, 190, 191. *See also* Tariff Act (1930); tariffs
travel
air, 90
cross-country, 63–68
See also railroads
Treasury, U.S., 170, 172, 216
Tribble, Tom, 59, 80
Trout, John P., 60

trucks/trucking, 97–102, 156
Truman, Harry, 189
Trump, Donald, 218
Tugwell, Rexford, 10, 49, 141, 142, 143, 171, 203

Umbarger, Walter Martin, 159
unemployment. *See* employment
United Auto Workers (UAW), 172, 179
United States
and detaining of Germans during World War I, 73
future of, 225
and improvements in people's lives, 192–99
population/demographics of, 3, 8, 63, 213
Simon analysis of advances in, 214–15
wealth and creature comforts in, 195, 213–15
as world's banker, 191
United Steelworkers, 172
United Telephone Company, 75
U.S. Steel, 33, 185
utilities, 36
utopianism, 223

Valentine brothers' grain elevator (Whiteland), 5, 50, 51–52, 83, 105, 144, 209
Veatch, Bill, 87
Vehorn, "Fats," 60
villages. *See* small towns

Wabash Line Railroad, 108
wages, 7, 32, 38, 59, 126, 127, 149, 158, 171
Wagner Act. *See* National Labor Relations Act
Wall Street. *See* banks/bankers
Wall Street Journal, xii, 149, 173, 180–81, 217
Wallace, Henry, 141
Washington Post, 40
wealth/wealthy
and blame for adversity, 207–8
explanation of America's rise to, 213–14
stealing from the, 58
taxes on, 35, 36
Wendt, Mary Carolyn Sharp, 25, 128, 130, 131–32, 143, 222
wheat, 142–43, 144
wheelbarrow, coins in, 79
Whippersnapper, Jack, 89
Whiteland Barn, 86–87
Whiteland Cafe, 73, 159
Whiteland High School: Class of 1930 at, 58–59

ABOUT THE AUTHOR

GEORGE MELLOAN HAD a long career as a writer and editor at *The Wall Street Journal*. He started as a reporter in Chicago, moved to Detroit to cover the auto industry, became Cleveland bureau manager in 1960 and in the following year was appointed Atlanta bureau manager, covering the racial strife that accompanied school desegregation in the South. He then moved to the Page One desk in New York, editing front-page "leaders." From 1966 to 1970, he was a foreign correspondent based in London, covering such stories as the Six-Day War in Israel, the Biafran war in Nigeria, and efforts at economic reform in the Soviet Union.

Mr. Melloan returned to New York in 1970 and joined the *Journal* editorial page staff, becoming deputy editor in 1973 with responsibility for daily operations under editor Robert Bartley. He and his wife, Joan, authored a book, *The Carter Economy*, published by John Wiley & Sons in 1978, correctly forecasting the economic stagnation that would result from price controls and inflationary policies. In 1987, he originated the op-ed column "Business World" to give more editorial-page attention to such issues as hostile takeovers of corporations.

In 1990, Mr. Melloan moved to Brussels to manage the *Journal*'s editorial pages in Europe and Asia, launching another new column, "Global View." Back in New York in 1994, he added the Americas to his responsibilities. He retired from the *Journal* in 2006 but still contributes op-eds and book reviews.

In 2009, he authored *The Great Money Binge: Spending Our Way to Socialism* (Simon & Schuster), a book describing the federal policies that led up to the 2008 market crash and recession. His next book, a history of *Journal* editorial-page thought, is expected to appear in 2017.

Mr. Melloan is a member of the New York Council on Foreign Relations and the Dutch Treat Club. He was winner of the Gerald Loeb award for distinguished business and financial journalism in 1981, the Daily Gleaner award of the Inter American Press Association twice in the 1980s for his writings about Soviet inroads in Latin America, and the *American Spectator*'s Barbara Olson award for excellence and independence in journalism in 2006. His home is in Westfield, N.J.